Pharisaism and Christianity

By Hugo Odeberg

TRANSLATED BY J. M. MOE

Concordia Publishing House

Saint Louis

Acknowledgment

I am grateful to Concordia Publishing House for the invitation to translate Professor Hugo Odeberg's book and for the publication of this translation.

I owe a special debt of thanks to Dr. John P. Milton, professor of Old Testament at Luther Theological Seminary, St. Paul, Minnesota, who was kind enough to go through the first half of my manuscript with me, and to Dr. Jacob Tanner, professor of religion at Waldorf College, Forest City, Iowa, who went through the second half of the manuscript. Both of these men made important corrections and assisted in revision of many parts of the manuscript.

October 27, 1962
Concordia College
Moorhead, Minnesota

J. M. Moe

TABLE OF CONTENTS

Table of Contents

Introduction: The Fundamental Question

The Relation Between
Pharisaism and Christianity

From the original New Testament records it is
clearly evident that the founders of Christianity as
well as the first Christian congregations found themselves in sharpest antithesis to the leaders in Judaism.
If one will consider these original records, that is,
the New Testament writings, as sources for our
knowledge of primitive Christianity, one cannot possibly deny this sharp antithesis. And whence should
one gain any knowledge of primitive Christianity if
not from the writings of primitive Christianity? As
a matter of fact, we possess no other primary sources.
From these sources we gather that the antithesis
between Christianity and Pharisaism was a fundamental one and was so interpreted by both parties.
It was an antithesis — one might properly say an
enmity — which was reflected in external and periph-
eral matters, so that, for example, one party denied
the other the right of guidance and instruction or
that the antithesis had its basis in inner competition
for influence upon the people. But antithesis between Jesus and the Pharisees, between Paul and
Judaism, also involved the extreme basic principles,
teachings, and experiences upon the recognition or

6

denial of which the entire existence of society was dependent. Expressed in other terms, this antithesis is historically conditioned, so that one might suppose that a reconciliation could be effected through a modification of Judaism or a development of Christianity or that both should recognize each other as different possibilities of dealing with reality. But the antithesis is also fundamental in the sense that a Pharisaism which assumes Christian lines of thought ceases to be Pharisaism, and a Christianity which incorporates Pharisaic lines of thought likewise ceases to be Christianity.

It is apparent also from the history of both these faiths that one must constantly keep in mind this irreconcilable antithesis and that one must above all strive to preserve the individuality of each. Particularly Christianity has repeatedly been in danger of incorporating Pharisaical lines of thought, and the great fathers of the church have always stressed the fact the Pharisaism is not something that can be combined with Christianity, but something that, if it is permitted to extend its influence, will work as a deadly poison which is bound to destroy the Christian life. Thus Luther, like no one else, took up Paul's battle against Pharisaism and vigorously pursued it.

In spite of this, in scholarly discussions as well as in homiletic instruction and in the treatment of Scripture, this antithesis has been a constant problem until this day, and will no doubt continue to be.

It is necessary again and again to seek to make clear what this antithesis is, or wherein it consists. We must constantly strive anew to familiarize ourselves with this antithesis, even as we must constantly strive for life itself.

It is important to emphasize that in the following presentation it is not a question of comparing Christianity and *Judaism* or of pitting the one against the other, but it is a question of Pharisaism and Christianity. In this matter two points of view should be kept in mind: (1) When it is a question of Jesus' opposition to Pharisaism, this is not synonymous with opposition to Judaism or Israel. There were in Israel tendencies and types of piety to which Jesus was not opposed, such as, for example, the devout circles known as "the quiet in the land," the so-called Jewish mysticism, and such individuals as Zechariah, Nathanael, and others. There were two principal factors in Israel's piety which He declared to be divine gifts: the Holy Scriptures, delivered to Israel, and the worship service of the synagog. (2) The Pharisaism in question is the Pharisaism against which Jesus warns as a danger *within* the Christian church. Jewish Pharisaism is significant as that form of Pharisaic tendency which obtained in Israel and of which it is important to give a fair and accurate picture in order to understand what Jesus assails in the Pharisaic tendency and what He warns against. It is not, then, an indictment either against Pharisaism in Israel or — even less — against Judaism, but it is the Pharisaic "leaven" within the *Christian* church against which Jesus warns and from which He wants to preserve His church.

Characterizations
of the
Antithesis
Between
Pharisaism
and
Christianity

The Theory that There Is No
Essential Antithesis

It might be well, first of all, to say something concerning the different ways of approaching this antithesis.

First may be mentioned the view that on the whole there is no essential difference between the teaching of Jesus and the doctrines of the leaders of the Pharisees, that is, the teachings of the rabbis. This is a view maintained above all by the more recent so-called Jewish liberals. Among others may be mentioned the English Jew, C. G. Montefiore. He has compiled a large work on the Synoptic Gospels in which he attempts to prove step by step and verse by verse that all the teachings of Jesus are to be found in the utterances of the rabbis, at any rate those teachings and words of Jesus which really are of any significance. He, of course, admits that there are some utterances of Jesus that do not have a counterpart in the rabbinical writings, but says that these utterances are all such as have no connection with reality; they are fantastic and eccentric and even the Christians themselves could never apply them to practical life. One ought to beware of lightly brushing aside this view of the Jewish scholars or of regarding it as merely a curiosity. On the contrary, it is most instructive. And the interpretations of these scholars are also full of correct observations. In reality there is no major difference between the teachings of the Pharisees and those of Jesus *as they later are generally interpreted and systematized in the scientific and homiletical exposition.*

The observations of the Jewish scholars have the great value of compelling us to direct our attention to the actual differences between Jesus and the rabbis as well as between Christianity and Pharisaism. For it is self-evident that so fundamental an antithesis as the one to which the history and original records of these two forms of religion testify would be inexplicable if the activity of Jesus had consisted in nothing more than to proclaim, in the main, what the Pharisees proclaimed. Thus the familiar word of Jesus in which He permits the disciples to practice what the Pharisees said, but not what they did (Matt. 23:3) has sometimes been misunderstood. If this were the only word of Jesus concerning the Pharisees that were preserved for us, it might properly be interpreted to mean that Jesus had censured only the conduct of the Pharisees. However, we have numerous utterances of Jesus which are aimed at the fundamental doctrines of the Pharisees. If it were permissible in this way to wrest a single word out of its context to support one's opinion, then one could with equal right insist that Paul was a great preacher of justification by the Law because he declared that the Law is holy and good. (Rom. 7:12)

We must therefore assert: if by comparing the utterances of the rabbis and those of Jesus we can find no greater differences between them, this is due to the fact that either the one or the other has been erroneously interpreted. Concretely viewed, the attempt at such comparisons actually made in more recent times affords little evidence of erroneous interpretations of the utterances of the Pharisees. It would then appear necessary to conclude that it is the utterances of Jesus which have been misinterpreted. And if this new interpretation of the words of Jesus is so easily adapted to the doctrines of the Pharisees, this is precisely an indication that one has already absorbed so much of the Pharisaical way of thinking that one is *no longer able to think as a Christian.* And such is actually the case. There are handbooks and textbooks in Christian ethics which might more properly serve as handbooks in Jewish ethics. It goes without saying that they have little in common with the ethics of primitive Christianity and the ethics of Luther.

*An Arbitrary Picture
of Pharisaism Which Does Not Conform
to Reality*

Another way of approaching the difference between Christianity and Pharisaism is the following.

It is admitted that this antithesis does in fact exist. The fundamental Christian principles are emphasized, and an attempt is made to define them precisely. Thereupon an ethical and a religious view is constructed which forms the direct opposite of the Christian view which has just been defined, and the conclusion is drawn that this is precisely what the Pharisaic view must have been, since Pharisaism was the antithesis of Christianity. However, the Pharisaism thus constructed is shown, upon closer examination, to be the very opposite of Pharisaism. Here we really deal with a case entirely analogous to the one described earlier. What is depicted as Christianity is not Christianity but Pharisaism.

How are we to account for this? Clearly by the fact that the Pharisaical ways of thinking have become natural for us without our being aware that they are Pharisaical. And what appears to us natural and reasonable is assumed — if one highly esteems the name of Christianity — as something self-evident in Christianity. We cannot and will not suppose — if we regard Christianity as the supreme religion — that the ideals set up by Christianity can be different from those we set up as the reasonable and the best. The only error is that these ideals have not derived from Christianity but from Christianity's antithesis: from Pharisaism. The result is that we confuse Christianity with Pharisaism and, while professing to be Christians, actually espouse Pharisaism.

The only proper method of establishing the true

difference between Christianity and Pharisaism is obviously that we seek to obtain as accurate a knowledge of both as we possibly can, and it is especially important that we gain a correct knowledge of the doctrines and fundamental principles of Pharisaism. *A true knowledge of Pharisaism is of fundamental importance for the protection of the unique character of Christianity.*

The Erroneous View that the Ethics of Pharisaism Is Merely Casuistic. Love of Mankind Is the Supreme Norm

In order to illustrate this, it may suffice to call attention to a few individual examples of mistaken antitheses between Christian and Jewish ethics and over against them to present the actual theories of Pharisaism. The following, for example, has been argued: In Pharisaism, or — which is the same thing — in normative Judaism, there is said to be only a casuistic ethics, a number, or more correctly an endless number, of ordinances which are to be obeyed solely because they are given by God. Such an assertion, however, is by no means in accord with the theory of Pharisaism. On the contrary, from the very beginning rabbinical instruction has as its purpose to discover the fundamental norms to which all the commandments could be traced.

We are familiar with the story of the pagan who

came to the great teacher of the Law, Hillel, and said to him: "If you can teach me the whole Law while I stand on one foot, you will make me a convert." Hillel made him a convert. He said: "Thou shalt love thy neighbor as thyself; and what is hateful to you, you shall not do to others. This is the whole Law; everything else is application." The usual rabbinical statement concerning the supreme norm is: "The fundamental thesis in the *Torah* (the Law) lies in the statement 'Thou shalt love thy neighbor as thyself.'"

"The Golden Rule" in its negative formulation appears already in *Tobit* 4:15: "What you yourselves do not wish that others should do to you, that you may not do to others." One must not draw any far-reaching conclusions from the fact that the Golden Rule in its Pharisaic form is negative, whereas in Jesus' Sermon on the Mount it is positive. For with the Pharisees the negative formulation is actually bound up with the positive: "Thou shalt love thy neighbor as thyself," and is nothing but a sequel to it. It is also worthy of note that we find the positive formulation even in a Jewish writing and the negative also in a primitive Christian writing. In the Jewish writing *The Second Book of Enoch* (Ch. 61:1) we read: "My children, keep your hearts from every injustice and from doing injury to any living creature whom the Lord has created. Just as a man prays to God for something for his own soul, so let him do to every living soul."

And in the Christian writing *The Teaching of the Twelve Apostles* (The *Didache*) 1:2, the proposition has this formulation: "Whatever you want people to refrain from doing to you, you must not do to them." In the Pharisaic view it was self-evident that right conduct did not consist either in something only positive or in something only negative, but every duty must include something one should do as well as something that, as a result thereof, one should not do. The main thing is that here all positive and negative commandments are combined in the proper social relationship: love for one's neighbor, including justice and mercy.

Countless examples might be cited to show how the importance of deriving all divine commandments (ethical duties) from one governing norm was stressed, as well as the importance of ascertaining that this norm was also actually morally and religiously the highest one. In this way, love of one's neighbor appeared in some way or other as the highest governing norm.

In *The Sayings of the Fathers* (Aboth, often called Pirke Abot) 2:13 ff., it is told:

> Rabbi John, the son of Zacchaeus, said to his five most intimate disciples: "Answer this question: What is the best a man ought to strive for?" Rabbi Elieser said: "A good eye"; Rabbi Joshua said: "A good associate"; Rabbi Jose said: "A good neighbor"; Rabbi Simeon said: "He that regards the result of an action"; Rabbi

Eleazar said: "A good heart." Then Rabbi John said to them: "I prefer the words of Eleazar ben Arach to your words, for your words are included in his."

The meaning is that he who lays claim to a good heart as the highest goal also realizes the other claims and that by the grace of God he receives every other good.

A most instructive example of the methodical search for superior norms engaged in by the teachers of the Pharisees is found in the following tradition recorded in the *Talmud:*

The *Torah* (that is, the five books of Moses) contains 613 precepts, of which 248 are positive and 365 negative. King David summed up all of these in 11 principles, namely, those found in Psalm 15, where we read:

Lord, who shall abide in Thy tabernacle? Who shall dwell in Thy holy hill? He that walketh uprightly, and worketh righteousness, and speaketh the truth in his heart. He that backbiteth not with his tongue, nor doeth evil to his neighbor, nor taketh up a reproach against his neighbor. In whose eyes a vile person is contemned, but he honoreth them that fear the Lord. He that sweareth to his own hurt and changeth not. He that putteth not out his money to usury nor taketh reward against the innocent. He that doeth these things shall never be moved.

The prophet Isaiah summed them up in six principles: "He that walketh righteously and speaketh uprightly, he that despiseth the gain of oppressions, that shaketh his hands from holding of bribes, that stoppeth his ears from hearing of blood and shutteth his eyes from seeing evil, he shall dwell on high." (Is. 33:15, 16a)

The prophet Micah reduced them to three principles: "He [God] hath shewed thee, O man, what is good. And what doth the Lord require of thee but to do justly, and to love mercy, and to walk humbly with thy God?" (Micah 6:8)

Later Isaiah again reduced them to two principles: "Keep ye judgment, and do justice." (Is. 56:1)

Finally, the prophets Amos and Habakkuk reduced them to one principle: "Seek ye Me, and ye shall live" (Amos 5:4); "The just shall live by his faith" (Hab. 2:4). (Babylonian Talmud Makkot 23b, 24a)

These are samples of the utterances of early Pharisaism. However, the insistence upon a supreme moral norm characterizes the entire history of rabbinical ethics. And this supreme norm is found, as stated, in love for one's neighbor, in the social virtues, in the Golden Rule — positive and negative — at least in theory. And it is with the theory that we are concerned in such a comparison. The practical performance leaves enough to be desired on the part of Christian and Pharisee alike.

It is worthy of note that the commandment or

norm concerning love for one's neighbor is the one which interprets all the other duties and commandments. This is the proper consequence of the fact that it is interpreted as the supreme norm. There is no doubt, then, that an essentially erroneous picture of Pharisaism is presented when, as often happens, its antithesis to Christianity is stated thus: "For the Christian, love is regarded as the highest, and other subordinate duties must give way to the commandment of love and mercy. For Pharisaism, all commandments are alike, so that the Pharisees cannot permit anyone to help his neighbor if he thereby breaks, for example, the Sabbath commandment."

Pharisaism is far more consistent in its thinking. It holds that ethical perfection is something that is set before man as a duty and consequently as a possibility. The ethical "right" is not something that is wholly isolated from reality, but something that is united with, and is a part of, the reality men live in. This reality emanates wholly from God and is determined by Him. Thus every ethical demand is a factor in an ethical context of wholeness which corresponds to reality. It is this ethical context of wholeness — *corpus ethicum* — which is also called God's Law. As in God's ordered world the forces of nature cooperate and balance one another in perfect harmony, even so with the different commandments in God's Law, that is, the various duties with which men are confronted. As the will of God is the soul in this world, so it is the soul in the ethical context. And God wills what is good. The righteous person, that is, he who at all times does what is right, has, by doing what is right, made himself a part of the order of God's perfect world. He himself and all his actions occupy their absolutely rightful place in reality, just as do all other forces. Since now the will of God, that is, His goodness or love, permeates the world and the ethical context, it is self-evident that all commandments and duties can be explained from love; and since love is always directed toward an object, love for one's neighbor becomes that from which the duties can be interpreted.

From this harmony between the worlds of reality and of duty it follows that theoretically no clash between duties will ever occur. Consequently the chief commandment, which is love for one's neighbor, can never — theoretically viewed — come into conflict with any other commandment. In other words, it is theoretically possible in every moment and in every situation to fulfill perfectly all commandments in question. Practically speaking, situations may arise which appear to be clashes between duties, but this is only on account of man's inability to comprehend the situation in which he lives. In such instances practical directions could be given whereby we find that the Pharisees always gave preference to the duty of loving one's neighbor. This duty must always be given due consideration. It is well to note, however, that in case of such an apparent clash of duties, one will always endeavor in one way or another to fulfill all the conflicting duties. This has often been referred to as something particularly absurd and is regarded as an artifice for fulfilling the commandments as easily as possible. Actually, the reason for this is to be found in a consistent and logical line of thought. Inasmuch as all the commandments spring from one and the same motive, and inasmuch as their fulfillment serves one and the same purpose, to neglect one commandment in favor of another is tantamount to neglecting a commandment for the sake of one's own advantage. Thus in any given situation the chief and governing commandment cannot be fulfilled unless all the other commandments that have a bearing on a situation are fulfilled.

We therefore find this theory consistently maintained, that — when, practically speaking, an apparent clash of duties is dealt with — the practical directions always insist that the claim upon the social duty of love for humanity must be fully satisfied. In exceptional cases one may refer to one commandment as "thrusting aside" another. Thus it is said, for instance, that the duty of saving a human life sets aside the Sabbath commandment. Reference is made to the Old Testament statement: "Ye shall keep My statutes and My judgments, which if a man do, he shall live in them" (Lev. 18:5) with the declaration of principle: "The purpose of the divine commandments is that we may live by them and not that we may die by them" (Babyonlian Talmud Yoma 85b). All the commandments serve the preservation of life in its highest sense, and the fulfillment of any commandment must never have as a consequence something which injures life. The preservation of life in its highest sense, however, becomes tantamount to love for one's neighbor. Consequently, in every situation, love for one's neighbor becomes the supreme commandment and gives content to all other commandments.

The same principle concerning the unity and mutual harmony of reality and ethics is given expression in the characteristic precision of the Pharisees in the following statement: "Rabbi Akiba said: 'The supreme and inclusive norm *(kelal gadol)* of the Law is this: Thou shalt love thy neighbor as thyself.' Ben Azzai said: 'Even more important is this epitome: This is the teaching concerning Adam's family: When God created men, He created them in the image of God" (Sifra on Lev. 19:18). That is to say: the ethical reality, like the created world, has its ultimate foundation in the nature of God. Love for one's neighbor is godlikeness and the objective of the world plan.

This is why the commandment of love is frequently cited together with a reference to the image of God in man. Therefore, in principle, this commandment includes all men. It is a Pharisaic principle that "neighbor" in the commandment, "Thou shalt love thy neighbor as thyself," embraces all men, even sinners and idolaters (that is, non-Jews). We read: "If one is not permitted to despise the stones in God's altar, which can apprehend neither good nor evil, how much less are we permitted to despise our fellowman, who bears within him the image of God" (Mekhilta on Ex. 20:26). "When do the blessings of God become your portion? When you walk in God's ways. Which, then, are God's ways? He is merciful, showing mercy even toward sinners; He nourishes all that He has created. In like manner you shall do good to one another. God is gracious, remembering with His kindness all who know Him and all who do not know Him. In this manner shall you also remember one another" (Tanna debe Eliyahu 26). "He who helps his fellowman has, as it were, received God" (Palestinian Talmud, Erubin X 5:1). "If your enemy hungers, give him bread; if he thirst, give him water." (Midrash Mishele 27)

"If man neglects the commandment to love one's neighbor, the result is that he also violates the other commandments, such as, 'Thou shalt not hate,' 'Thou shalt not seek revenge,' 'Thou shalt not bear a grudge because of a wrong.' Then he also transgresses the commandment: 'Thy brother shall live with thee.' If he transgresses these commandments, it is as if he had committed murder" (Sifre on Deut. 19:11). In the final analysis the preservation of life is love, and injury to life is to kill.

In these two opposites, love and death, the subjective and the objective are summed up in a remarkable manner. The highest form of life, the preservation of life in its highest potency, may be said to be love, that is, a life in which can be seen nothing but kindness and love. This, however, takes place by practicing love. Love for one's neighbor, the love directed toward others, toward one's neighbor and toward mankind, is thus the highest in reality as well as the highest ethical commandment. Thus, in the theory of Pharisaism, life's highest form is conceived as love for mankind. In other words, life's supreme form is to love one's neighbor. Correspondingly, to entirely neglect the duty of love and to do the opposite is, of course, in its extreme implication, identical with murdering one's neighbor. However, this is also identical with the destruction of one's own life: death. He who loves lives in the fullest sense; he who does the opposite is dead. In this manner the selfish factor disappears from the ethics of Pharisaism in the striving for one's own perfection.

It is therefore understandable when a Jewish scholar, Samson Hochfeld, believes that he can characterize the ethical principle of Judaism in contrast to the contemporary Greek thinkers as follows:

> To the constructive achievements of Judaism belongs the recognition of one's fellowmen and thereby of mankind. The concern of the non-Jewish thinkers of antiquity is directed toward the ego. The question as to the welfare of others is asked only in passing. "What is the

object of human life?" is the basic ethical problem for the Greek philosophers. "Happiness," they reply; and according to their varying points of view, they prescribe different ways of attaining this happiness: the mastery of reason over the instincts, pleasure, material security, peace of mind. Not one of them, however, has found the answer: "You will find happiness by making your fellowman happy, by doing good to him, by helping him, by lightening life's burden for him." In other words, the non-Jewish ethic of antiquity is thoroughly egotistically oriented; it is an individual ethic for which the great questions of social ethics remain alien. Only the Bible has introduced one's fellowmen as a necessary factor in the ethical consideration and has elevated the welfare of one's fellow mortals to the norm for appraising human conduct.

When the Gospel of St. Matthew (23:23) relates that Jesus censures the Pharisees and the scribes for tithing mint and dill and cummin, but neglecting the weightier matters of the Law, namely, justice and mercy and faith, adding: "These ought ye to have done, and not to leave the other undone," one would have to say — if one places these words in the light of the Pharisees' own theory — that Jesus here upbraids the Pharisees with regard to principles which to them should have been obvious. The statement, "These ought ye to have done, and not to leave the other undone," is in reality a brief and striking summary of the Pharisaic principles described above to the effect that the different commandments could not invalidate one another, inasmuch as they all have the same basic aim, but in fulfilling the commandments the important matter is always that precisely this basic aim shall be maintained. The basic aim is, as stated, the social duty which may be characterized as love for one's fellowmen, or, in the words of Jesus, "justice and mercy and faith." The background for this rebuke of Jesus, therefore, is not to be found in any ethical theory of the Pharisees which would place insignificant ceremonial precepts on an equality with the great commandment concerning justice and mercy. The background is found in something else. This, however, we cannot designate in more detail until we understand the true antithesis, the actual differences, between the ethics of Jesus and Pharisaic morality.

The Erroneous View that Pharisaism Is Not the Ethics of Character

Another difference which is wrongly set up between Pharisaic and Christian ethics is that the decisive factor for Pharisaism is said to be the actual fulfillment of the demand of the Law, while Christianity, on the other hand, is said to lay greater stress on the importance of the attitude of the mind. The Pharisaic theory teaches us something different. The teachers of Pharisaism emphasize throughout that what matters is the will itself. For example, the circumstance that Israel is the chosen people is declared to be contingent upon the fact that Israel at Mount Sinai declared itself to be ready to obey God and to assume the responsibility of the Law ("the yoke of heaven"), while the other peoples refused to do so. A pagan people may perform God's will while Israel is disobedient; but the heathen people do not on this account possess the Lord's favor, while Israel, who has forfeited His favor, does possess His favor because Israel possesses the right will and the proper attitude of mind.

Pharisaism is indeed far more lenient in its appraisal of the moral life than is Christianity, and this precisely because it attaches such great significance to the right attitude of the mind. One need not be unduly anxious because of one's sins against the divine will if one has once determined to do what is right. For God is merciful, indulgent, and gracious, and He Himself supplies what may be lacking on the part of men seeking righteousness in the matter of fulfilling the moral duty. "If a man had the intention of performing a duty, but was hindered therein, the Scriptures reckon it as if he had performed it; this is the essential meaning of the Prophet Malachi's words 'them that thought upon His name.'" (Babylonian Talmud, Berakhot 6a)

It might be said that the difference between Christianity and Pharisaism is altogether the reverse. The Christian looks upon the divine demands as something absolute. The Law has not led to righteousness, and no one can escape the wrath of God. Here there is no difference between the one who says yes and the one who says no; both are sinners and are without excuse (Rom. 1:18–2:24). Therefore the Christian knows that salvation is necessary. The Pharisee cannot conceive of this necessity, since he knows that, after all, God is merciful if men only possess the right will.

A Christianity which has been influenced by Pharisaism may also experience difficulties with respect to the central Christian doctrine of Christ as the Savior. It lacks the possibility of understanding that Jesus needs to be something other than one who correctly proclaims the will of God. That a merciful and loving God should send a Savior into the world for the sake of men appears to it as an unnecessary and irrational detour, inasmuch as God by Himself is both able to forgive man and to support him in his continued moral endeavors.

The Error of Classifying Pharisaical Ethics as One of Reward and Punishment

The same applies to other assumptions that have been made with regard to Pharisaism, as, for example, when an attempt has been made to see in it the antithesis of what was presumed to be something self-evident in Christianity. It has been said that Pharisaism preaches obedience to the divine demands merely from fear of punishment or the hope of reward. Both of these, however, in point of principle, have most vigorously been denied by the Pharisees. An act, a deed, is pleasing to God or ethically worthy only if it is done for the sake of God, or, as it is also stated, for its own sake, that is, for the sake of the good itself. And it should be observed that, in Pharisaic language, "for the sake of God," or "for the sake of heaven," means exactly the same as "for the sake of the good." God wills something because it is good and not the other way around. For this reason the leaders of the Pharisees can declare: "He who does not perform the good for the sake of the good, for him it were better that he had not been born" (Babylonian Talmud, Berakhot, 17a). Or: "Whatever you do, you must do for the sake of heaven" (Sifre on Deut. 11:13). Or: "It is immaterial whether one does much or little just so he does it for the sake of God (or: has his thoughts directed toward heaven)" (*ächad ham-marbä weächad ham-ma-mi̇̈t ubilbad sä-jekavven libba lassámajim* — Babylonian Talmud Berakhot 5b 17a). A statement from the Pharisaic doctrines frequently quoted in rabbinical writings is the following: "Be not like servants who serve a master thinking of reward, but be like servants who serve a master without thinking of reward" (Abot 1:3). "The reward of a good deed is the good deed, and the reward of a sin is a sin" (Abot 4:2). On this point Pharisaism is positive and precise.

The Pharisaic viewpoint on the question of reward and punishment as an ethical motive is clearly developed in later rabbinism, which in this as well as in most instances may be regarded as the continuation and cultivation of Pharisaism. The rabbinical point of view on the question is clearly and unequivocally defined in statements such as the following by the great Jewish teacher and philosopher Maimonides in his *Mishnah Torah,* Hilkhot Teshubot 9:1:

> Men are not permitted to say: "I will fulfill the commandments of the Law and occupy myself with its wisdom in order that I may receive all the blessings promised in the Law, or in order that I may receive eternal life; and I will keep aloof from sin in order to escape the misery which the Law threatens to inflict as a punishment and in order that I may not forfeit eternal life." One is not permitted to serve God in this manner, for he who serves God in such a way does so merely from fear of Him. This is not the viewpoint of the prophets, nor of the Wisdom writers. He who serves God out of love occupies himself with the Law and the commandments and walks in the way of wisdom, not for the sake of profit, or from fear of misfortune, or to gain happiness, but he serves the truth because it is truth.

There would be more reason to say that Christianity to a certain extent adopts the morality of reward than to say this about Pharisaism. For in the Sermon on the Mount we find a reference to the reward in heaven, the reward with the Father, as a motive for one's actions. "Take heed that ye do not your alms before men, to be seen of them; otherwise ye have no reward of your Father which is in heaven" (Matt. 6:1). "When thou doest alms, let not thy left hand know what thy right hand doeth; that thine alms may be in secret; and thy Father which seeth in secret Himself shall reward thee openly" (Matt. 6:3, 4). "Pray to thy Father which is in secret, and thy Father which seeth in secret shall reward thee openly" (Matt. 6:6). "When thou fastest, anoint thine head, and wash thy face; that thou appear not unto men to fast, but unto thy Father which is in secret; and thy Father, which seeth in secret, shall reward thee openly." (Matt. 6:17, 18)

It may be noted that the Pharisees may use the word "reward" in connection with duties which had been accomplished or in connection with good works. "Reward," however, really means the necessary satisfying result of the deed. It is often said that the heathen, the ungodly, receives the reward of his good deeds already in this life, while the godly receives it only in heaven, with God. This corresponds with the expression in the Sermon on the Mount, "They have their reward," and, "have reward of your heavenly Father." In Pharisaism, however, the reward is not used as a motive for action.

The Error that Pharisaical Ethics Is a Doctrine of Merit

The same applies to the assertion that Pharisaical ethics is a doctrine of merit, that is, that the Pharisees permitted the good man to reckon to himself his good deeds as having special merit before God. According to Pharisaic belief, man owes thanks to the grace of God that he has any capacity at all for doing good. The story of the Pharisee in the temple, recorded in St. Luke 18, is completely faithful to this picture. The Pharisee is here described as one who *thanks God* because He granted him the ability to abstain from the vile manner of life indulged in by sinners. The liturgy of the Jewish worship service is replete with such prayers of thanksgiving. But never has the Pharisaic theory permitted the pious man to attribute merit *to himself* by his obedience to the Law.

Always it is God alone who attributes merit to a man, declaring him to be *zakkai* (worthy). God thereby grants him something which he himself has not deserved, and still less something which he can lay claim to for his own account. "The prisoner is not able to liberate himself from prison" (Babylonian Talmud, Berakhot 5b), says the parable.

The Pharisaic Concept
of "Zakut"

A word generally translated "merit" appears frequently in Pharisaical and rabbinical pronouncements. It is the word *zakut*. *Zakut*, however, does not have the same meaning as religious merit or merit per se. The actual, original meaning is "innocence," to be or to have been found innocent of something one is accused of. *Zakut*, then, means about the same as "possessing the right," to have the right on one's side. From this usage the word has developed in the direction of meaning "to have been found to possess greater right." Thus, one who has passed through an ordeal and has been subjected to a test has received a *zakut*. Accordingly, when the thought is transported to the test to which men's ethical actions are subjected, *zakut* may be the expression of approval, approbation, the testimonial which this ethical action receives.

In whatever meaning the word may be taken, however, the point is always that *zakut* ("merit") is something attributed by another, and finally, of course, by God. To possess *zakut*, then, is to have been declared innocent, or to have been pronounced worthy, to have approval and commendation, to the best of one's ability to have received a special precedence of privilege.

The latter applies, above all, to the great religious figures of the past, to the "fathers." To their *zakut* one may refer. But, as stated, it is diametrically opposed to the Pharisaic theory to say that the individual himself should be permitted to appraise his own deeds, attributing to himself a *zakut,* a merit. The great difference between attributing *zakut* to others and attributing such to oneself, seen from the viewpoint of the Pharisees, perhaps appears most prominently by citing two statements. The one reads: "He who is occupied with the Torah for the love thereof merits many things; and not only so, but he is worth the whole world, as he is called friend, beloved, one who loves God and loves mankind,* makes glad both God and mankind" (Abot R. Meir, 6:1). Here, accordingly, what is involved is a statement *about* the righteous or the seeker after God. This statement, however, by no means implies that such a one should say of himself or have it said of himself: "I merit many things," etc. This fact appears from the following dictum: "Rabbi John, the son of Zacchaeus, used to say (it was his motto): 'If you have been much occupied with fulfilling the Torah, take no credit to yourself, for thereunto were you created.'" (Abot 2:8)

That it is not a question of the "worthy" one alleging his "worthiness," that is, his merit, also follows from the fact that humility and the inability to see one's own worth, one's merit, enters as a neces-

---

* At this point Odeberg renders it: "One who loves everything living."

sary factor in merit, in *zakut*. On the other hand, he who asserts his worthiness (that is, his merit) would thereby forfeit it. He who is most worthy is humble, and asks: "Have I any portion at all in the life of the world to come?" The passage in Abot 6:1, from which we just quoted, declares: "To be occupied with the divine Law clothes him who practices the Law with humility and the fear of God, making him qualified to be righteous, godly, and honest."

The Pharisaical Theory
of Merit

As already emphasized above, the narrative of the Pharisee and the publican in the temple, recorded Luke 18, is by no means in itself a caricature or a false picture of Pharisaic piety. This narrative, however, is certainly a caricature the way it is usually *expounded*. It is said that the Pharisee here pleads his merits before God and bases upon them a claim. However, nothing of the kind appears in the text. This is something which has been read into it because of a preconceived notion of how Pharisaism must have been in order that it should be in conflict with Christianity or the teaching of Jesus. The fact is that the text clearly points out that the Pharisee praises and thanks God because he, the Pharisee, is what he is. When he recounts what he himself does, this really implies, within the framework of such a thanksgiving, the praising of God. Such a thanksgiving is not essentially different from the thanksgiving which is offered to God by the men in the worship service of the synagog: "Praise be to Thee, Lord, our God, that Thou hast not created me to be a woman." As little as the man hereby asserts before God as a matter of personal merit that he is a man and not a woman, just as little does the pious Pharisee's thanksgiving to God for having saved him from the sinful life into which others unfortunately have fallen imply any assertion of personal merit before God. There is no fundamental difference between the Pharisee's prayer of thanksgiving and that which a Christian can offer up because he has been saved out of a life of sin. The fact that in both instances a good deal of conceit and self-admiration may creep in obviously has no significance for the comparison between Pharisaism and Christianity per se.

On the other hand, that a thanksgiving just like the one referred to in St. Luke 18:11 ff. could occur in the case of the Pharisees is shown by the quotations from rabbinical literature to which Billerbeck alludes in connection with St. Luke 18:11 in his *Kommentar zum Neuen Testament aus Talmud und Midrasch,* among which the following may be mentioned:

> When Rabbi Nechonja ben Hakkana left the Talmud school, he used to say: "I thank Thee, Lord, my God and the God of my fathers, that Thou hast granted me a portion among those

who spend their life in the school and in the synagog, and not those who frequent the circus and the theater. I work hard, and so do they; I am zealous, and so are they. I strive to attain Paradise, and they exert themselves to reach the pit of perdition" . . . (Palestinian Talmud, Berakhot IV 2, 29b)

This comment is made in connection with Ps. 16: 10: "Thou dost not give me up to Sheol, or let Thy godly one see the Pit" (RSV). Thus we see that the strongest emphasis is laid on the fact that even the most virtuous manner of life is a gift from God.

The "Literal" Interpretation of the Moral Law

A completely erroneous view of the Pharisaic "doctrine of merit" has arisen through the fact that the Pharisaic performance of duty has been called literal, by which it is understood that the Pharisee regards it as sufficient that one fulfills a commandment according to the letter. Over against this alleged Pharisaic view have been put the demands which are set forth in the Sermon on the Mount, saying that Jesus instead demanded that the commandments should be fulfilled in their spiritual sense. According to this, the Pharisees stood on a lower plane of requirement than Jesus with regard to the fulfillment of the divine commandments.

The fundamental error of this view, of which even expert authorities on Pharisaism may become guilty, is that its proponents do not explain what they mean by the word "literal," but quite thoughtlessly use it first in one sense and then in another. In the modern, common usage of the word "literal," it denotes an interpretation which lays hold on only the verbal significance of a statement. By taking the commandment literally, "Thou shalt not kill" is taken to mean that it merely prohibits the actual taking of another's life. The literal sense, then, means practically the same as a strictly verbal sense, without any regard to the context, nuances, the underlying purpose, motive, and the like. However, this manner of taking a commandment literally is the very opposite of the literal interpretation to which the Pharisees devoted themselves. They would say: Here by no means do we have an interpretation according to the letter, but simply an interpretation according to the shallow meaning (Hebrew, *pesat*). And since "literal" in everyday parlance has once received this usage — to denote the verbal meaning — it would be better simply to restrict the use of the word to this popular usage. In this case one would have to say: The Pharisees are so far from accepting a "literal" interpretation of the commandment that it was one of the most intensively cultivated endeavors of the Pharisees to penetrate beyond the literal meaning, beyond the superficial, verbal content. All the enormous and vast study pursued by their scribes may be said to have concentrated on the effort to penetrate behind the mere superficial meaning of the words of Holy Scripture and to dis- cover all the underlying meanings contained therein.

The principle held by the Pharisees, which is erroneously called literal interpretation, implies that by giving attention to the formulation of an inspired utterance, its shades of meaning, its "sound," as it were, one desires to penetrate to all the wealth of its meaning. In other words, it is not enough to understand what a Scripture passage means "accord- ing to the words," on the surface, or, as the Pharisees express it, its *pesat*. Attention is therefore given to the letters and not only to the words. By noting the verbal sound one hopes to arrive at the deeper, the inner, the spiritual meaning, or the whole wealth of meanings. For the opinion was that a Spirit-given word had such a depth of meanings.

Now, it is possible to show that the "literal in- terpretation" of the Pharisees — which, as stated, is the direct opposite of literal interpretation in our sense — actually led them to the deeper understand- ing to which they aspired. The Pharisees have thus arrived at the view: "Hatred weighs just as much as idolatry, unchastity, or murder"; or: "He who hates his neighbor belongs to those who shed blood" (Derekh Eretz 9). It cannot be disputed that the Pharisees by no means supposed that the command- ment "Thou shalt not kill" was kept by refraining from killing another.

The Pharisaic "literal interpretation" is, of course, foreign to such contexts as are discussed here. It is, however, not as foreign to reality as may appear from the modern theological point of view. It is possible to assess this "literal interpretation" if one, instead of the Bible, considers some writings which in modern times are regarded as inspired, such as, for example, a poem. Surely everyone is willing to admit that a poem has something more to offer than the mere verbal meaning. The modern attitude toward utterances of the Bible may be compared to the attitude toward a work of poetry, which declares that a statement such as, "The sun sprinkles drops of crimson on the eastern skies," signifies nothing more than "the sun will soon rise." This is literal interpretation in the modern theological sense. But the Pharisaic view corresponds most closely to the one which maintains that in the phraseology of the poet there is to be found an infinite store of great value which reaches beyond the surface (the so-called literal) meaning.

The antithesis, then, between the righteousness demanded by Jesus and the righteousness of the Pharisees is not simply that the Pharisees were content with the superficial interpretation of the different commandments, while Jesus demanded a deeper penetration into their spiritual meaning.

At this point one might rather say that theoretically there is no distinction whatever between Jesus and the Pharisees. The only difference in the appli-

cation of the theoretical principle of the deeper
meaning of the commandments lies in the fact that
the Pharisees appear to give greater consideration
to the conditions of the practical life than does Jesus.
They were not less consequential in demanding that
a commandment be fulfilled in its deepest meaning,
but they endeavored to find a means whereby this
could also become practically realized. An unrestricted application of such rules as not resisting
a wrong inflicted, but turning the other cheek for
every blow, or without consideration giving to him
who asks, or not turning away from him who would
borrow, cannot, of course, be regarded as possible by
a Pharisee. He points out that this would be contrary to the rational fulfillment of the other commandments; and he can point out that even the most
self-confident Christian, who places the greatest demands upon himself and others, usually is not particularly willing to lend money even to a brother
and even less to endure insults, at any rate in such
instances where retaliation does not involve much
of a risk. He further points to the fact that the Christian readily strikes even though he himself has not
received any blow. On the other hand, as far as
possible to overlook personal injuries and to share
one's substance with those in need — this is something that Pharisaism forcibly stresses. Relating to
this matter there are extensive utterances to be
found, such as, for example, the following: "There
are four types of men. The average type says: 'What

is mine is mine and what is yours is yours.' The vulgar type says: 'What is mine is yours and what is yours is mine.' The pious type says: 'What is mine and what is yours are yours.' The wicked type says: 'What is yours and what is mine are mine.'" (Abot 5:10)

Such a dissimilarity as the one here alluded to — that Pharisaism with its precepts stays within the bounds of possibility and reason, while the precepts of Jesus, judging by their formulation, imply demands irrespective of the possibility of their practical fulfillment — does not, however, belong to the type of dissimilarities we have been concerned with thus far, namely, such as are usually presented in order to show that Christianity is superior to Pharisaism. For, on the contrary, evading the demands which lie outside the realm of possibility one would usually interpret the words of Jesus in such a way that they do not have the unrestricted range which they appear to have according to their phraseology. As the words of Jesus here under consideration are generally interpreted, there is no difference whatever between the demands of Jesus and those of the Pharisees, at any rate not such as would demonstrate that the demands of the Pharisees are less than those of Jesus.

With the above-mentioned differences which are wrongly set forth between Pharisaism and Christianity, the catalog of such differences is, of course, by no means exhausted. These examples, however, must suffice to justify the thesis that the very thing which is regarded as unique in Christianity or in Christian ethics is often precisely characteristic of Pharisaism and may therefore be said to constitute a Pharisaism under the name of Christianity.

The Actual
Antithesis
Between
Pharisaical and
Primitive
Christian Ethics

Illustrated by
a Specific Situation

If, on the other hand, we seek to discover the
actual, fundamental differences between Pharisaism
and Christianity, we can perhaps best do this by
calling attention to a situation described in the New
Testament writings where the Pharisaical interpretation actually appears in sharp opposition to the
Christian interpretation. The gospels as well as the
Pauline epistles abound in such situations. However, in John 8 we encounter a situation in which
the antithesis is emphasized with particular force.
There we read of a dispute between Jesus and the
Jews in which both parties occupy absolutely irreconcilable positions. Jesus says to the Pharisees:
"Ye are of your father the devil, and the lusts of
your father ye will do. He was a murderer from the
beginning, and abode not in the truth, because there
is no truth in him (John 8:44). The Pharisees reply:
"Now we know that Thou hast a devil" (John 8:52).
He who reads the entire passage can plainly see that
the issue does not involve idle vituperations, but that
the words are spoken by both parties in dead earnest.

We must, in the first place, inquire: What kind
of men are these opponents of Jesus, and what is

there about them that Jesus condemns them so vehe-
mently and without any reservation? First of all, we
must note that the narrative throughout is in accord
with the characteristics which we are able from the
Jewish sources to confirm among the Pharisees or
the rabbis. The Jews' reply to Jesus' questions and
allegations concerns the expressions and manner of
speaking which are in vogue among the Pharisees.
Without entering too much into details it may be
established that the concern here is with Jews *who
are in earnest about their piety and their observance
of the Law.* Or expressed in modern terms, they are
men *who entertain the loftiest ethical ideals and
who are in earnest about their moral claims and their
religious faith.*

These men cannot but feel that they are being
unjustly judged by Jesus. From their point of view
it appears that Jesus pronounces them devoid of the
very things which they particularly strive to possess,
and that He accuses them of the offenses and defects
which they very specially loathe and which they
know that they scrupulously avoid.

He tells them that there is a possibility that they
might be free if they learned to know the truth
(John 8:32). This statement implies, then, that the
Pharisees were not free and that they knew not the
truth. However, one of the pillars in the whole
Pharisaic way of thinking and in all their ethical
striving and preaching founded upon this way of

looking at things was that he who devoted his life entirely to performing the will of God as it is revealed in the Law thereby possessed the truth and was a free man. This was precisely what the Pharisees claimed to lay particular stress on, that to penetrate into God's Law means to discover the actual truth, and that to accommodate one's life according to the precepts, norms, and rules of God's Law is to be free. This was especially possible for Israel, which had entered into covenant with God to obey His Law, to be His people, and therefore to be free. This covenant had first entered into the life of the people through Abraham, and as the seed of Abraham the Pharisees were assuredly free, since they diligently studied the Law and sought to live up to its requirements. This is the meaning of the reply which the Jews in John 8:33 gave to the words of Jesus: "We be Abraham's seed, and were never in bondage to any man; how sayest Thou, Ye shall be made free?"

Jesus does not accept this reply, but calls attention to a truth which was as vital to the Pharisees as to every other moral enthusiast: "Whosoever committeth sin is the servant of sin" (John 8:34). According to Pharisaic view, an essential difference between one who is free and one who is a slave in the moral sense is that he who does right is free, and he who does wrong becomes a slave of his evil inclination. "Sin begins as a guest; later it becomes your master." (Genesis Rabbah 22:6; Babylonian

Talmud Sukkah 52b, Jalqut 2 Sam., No. 148). The Pharisees were convinced in their own minds that they were most conscientiously on guard lest sin should gain dominion over them, and also on guard that they might constantly admonish and warn others to be watchful likewise. Especially was attention called to the obligation incumbent upon an Israelite in view of the faithfulness to God and the covenant with God, which was inaugurated by their progenitor Abraham. By virtue of the fact that the Israelite was a child of Abraham he had an illustrious line of ancestors to look back upon both as an exhorting and as a sustaining example. The example of these ancestors exhorted him to cling to the covenant. To do wrong — to commit sin — was the same as breaking the covenant with God; it was to be unfaithful to Him and to serve someone else. Sin, then, becomes idolatry, identifying oneself with the heathen, who is a slave under idols. But the fathers, from Abraham on, are also a help. Their many and great virtues constitute a source of moral strength to their descendants, and are, as it were, meted out to them. They could be certain that none of the fathers had been unfaithful to God, "committed adultery with idols," as the prophets expressed it. They could know that the fathers had always done God's will and performed His work.

This is what the Pharisees stressed among themselves and others. And for this reason they must regard it as an especially unjust accusation when

Jesus upbraids them for not performing the works of their Father. They are convinced that all their thoughts and actions have as their object to prove that they are God's children, just as their fathers had been. Therefore they say: "We be not born of fornication; we have one Father, even God" (John 8:41). It is a declaration of the Pharisees that "the Israelites are beloved, for they are called children of God."

To this Jesus replies with the accusation which to Pharisaism was a dreadful one: "Ye are of your father the devil, and the lusts of your father ye will do. He was a murderer from the beginning and abode not in the truth, because there is no truth in him. When he speaketh a lie, he speaketh of his own; for he is a liar, and the father of it." (John 8:44)

Here, then, the irreconcilable antithesis between Jesus and the Pharisees is brought to its climax. They whose whole object and striving were aimed at doing the will of God are told that they are doing what their father the devil desired. They whose whole life was dedicated to inquiring into the truth, to doing the truth and teaching the truth, are told that they are like their father in whom there is no truth and who can speak only lies, yea, is the father of lies. They who suppose that they are endeavoring to lead men to eternal life are told that they are murderers and the children of murderers. In keeping with this their judgment of Jesus is also accentuated: "Say we not well that Thou hast a devil?" (John 8:48). From their point of view no other explanation was possible.

It is against the same background that Paul, the former Pharisee, declares concerning the Jews in Rom. 2:17-24: "Behold, thou art called a Jew, and restest in the Law, and makest thy boast of God, and knowest His will, and approvest the things that are more excellent, being instructed out of the Law; and art confident that thou art a guide of the blind, a light of them which are in darkness, an instructor of the foolish, a teacher of babes, which hast the form of knowledge and of the truth in the Law. Thou therefore which teachest another, teachest thou not thyself? Thou that preachest a man should not steal, dost thou steal? Thou that sayest a man should not commit adultery, dost thou commit adultery? Thou that abhorrest idols, dost thou commit sacrilege? Thou that makest thy boast of the Law, through breaking the Law dishonorest thou God? For the name of God is blasphemed among the Gentiles through you, as it is written." Paul here by no means refers to such people as were thieves and adulterers in the ordinary sense, but, on the contrary, to such as regarded these things as being far beneath them. Paul has in mind the "righteous," those who place rigorous demands upon themselves as well as upon others.

The Pharisees, then, regard themselves as those

whose whole endeavor is aimed at fulfilling the will of God and also at helping others obey the will of God, as those who require of themselves and others that their whole life shall be regulated by the will of God, that is, by righteousness and truth and mercy. Jesus, however, views these same people as those who are slaves under sin, who do not comprehend the truth, who are not able to recognize the voice of God nor to discern any message coming from the higher world, whose entire striving in reality is in line with the will of the devil, serving the purposes of evil, which issue at last in death instead of life, in destroying life instead of saving it. In such a situation lies the greatest conceivable antithesis between the two, Jesus and the Pharisees. Wherein, then, does this antithesis consist? What is there in the Pharisees that Jesus condemns so severely, and what is there in Jesus that the Pharisees are unable to accept or comprehend?

It is well to keep clearly in mind that what is the object of Jesus' censure and at the same time is the reason why the Pharisees (the Jews) regard themselves to be unjustly condemned and cannot possibly accept the viewpoint of Jesus, is this: The Pharisees are actually people whose life is wholly devoted to searching out the will of God, to carrying out this divine will, and to helping as many as possible to the same realization of God's will. We are forced, then, to the conclusion that the antithesis between Jesus and the Pharisees is seen in their earnest striving to discover the truth and to attain the highest ethical ideal.

If this characteristic of the Pharisees is overlooked, most of the conversation between them and Jesus in the eighth chapter of the Gospel of St. John becomes meaningless. On the other hand, it becomes replete with clear and significant content if we agree that the picture of the Pharisees here presented is the one implied by the conversation.

It deserves to be further noted that this conversation, according to the Gospel narrative, takes place between Jesus and Jews who "believed on Him" (John 8:31). That is to say, these Jews could accept what Jesus had previously said. It is in this conversation, then, that the irreconcilable antithesis appears for the first time. In the preaching of Jesus there must, therefore, have been something that the Pharisees could fully approve, so that they were led to the conviction (the "belief") that He was a spokesman of God and a true teacher. At the same time the Gospel would clearly emphasize that Jesus wished to impress upon these people that there was between their points of view an irreconcilable antithesis and that He could not accept them as His disciples.

This is not to say that from a Christian point of view they were really good people. On the contrary, we assume that Jesus was perfectly right in His severe denunciation of these men. There is every reason to suppose that from the Christian point of view, at any rate from Jesus' point of view, they were evil men. How had they become evil? The answer is: *Quite simply by having determined to become good.* While wanting to be just and pious and while seeking to attain this, they had become evil; while wanting to be God's children, they had become the children of the devil; while seeking to perform the works of God, they had come to perform the works of the devil. While earnestly striving to obey God's commands, they are incapable of discerning the voice of God. When they come face to face with the Messenger of God, they do not recognize Him, nor will they have anything to do with Him, even declaring Him to be possessed of an evil spirit.

Here a decisive difference between Pharisaism and Christianity comes to light. Pharisaism declares: Man *shall* will what is good, and he is *able* to will what is good. He who wills what is good and also seeks to do good becomes a good and upright person.

Christian ethics, however, is based on the understanding of man's true nature and declares: By nature man neither can nor will do what is good. If he directs his will and his efforts toward that which is good, he in reality comes to strive for that which is evil. He who endeavors to do what is good will do what is evil. For a corrupt tree cannot bear good fruit. And the evil person has become a corrupt tree, even though he himself would produce good fruit and believes that he is capable of doing so.

The Teaching of Pharisaism
Concerning the Free Will

That man's will with respect to morality is free
is a fundamental conviction of Pharisaism, a conviction which is expressed in the oldest as well as in
the most recent writings. Clear and unmistakable,
for example, is the testimony of Ecclesiasticus (15:
14 ff.):

> The Lord Himself made man from the begin-
> ning and left him to his free choice; if thou wilt,
> thou shalt keep the commandments; and to act
> with fidelity is a matter of liking. He hath set
> fire and water before thee; thou shalt stretch
> forth thy hand to whichever thou wilt. Before
> man is life and death, and whichever he liketh
> shall be given him. For the wisdom of the Lord
> is great, and He is mighty in power and be-
> holdeth all things; and His eyes are upon them
> that fear Him, and He knoweth every work of
> man. He commanded no one to be godless,
> and He gave no one license to sin.

So firmly convinced are they of the freedom of
the will in ethical matters, and so important is the
doctrine concerning it, that in behalf of it they even
sacrifice some of God's omnipotence. Everything is
in God's hands, but man's moral choice lies in his
own hands; of course, not as something which is to
his own credit but as a gift of God. For it is God
who has given man his free will and thereby the
possibility of doing good.

We read: "Rabbi Akiba used to say: 'All things

are foreseen, and free will is given, and the world is judged by goodness'" (Abot 3:19). "Everything is in God's hands except godliness" (Babylonian Talmud Megillah 25a; Berakhot 33b; Niddah 16b). At the origin of man the angel in charge of conception asks the Lord: "What shall be the fate of this seed? Shall it produce a strong man or a weak man, a wise man or a fool, a rich man or a poor man?" Whereas "wicked man" or "righteous man" he does not mention, for this is determined by man himself. (Babylonian Talmud Niddah 16b)

The choice of evil or unrighteousness is therefore called by the Pharisees "to give oneself up to a stranger," "to yield oneself to an alien service"; but never is this conceived as anything other than one's own free choice, although, as previously mentioned, a repeated choice of this kind may be regarded as something that will lead to bondage — yet not to a bondage which cannot be broken as soon as sufficient volition is exerted. "He who yields to his evil inclination is like one who serves an idol, for 'Thou shalt not permit any idol to have dominion over thee.'" (Palestinian Talmud Nedarim IX 1, 25a). "When the Israelites occupy themselves with the Torah and with acts of kindness, their evil inclination is mastered by them, not they by their evil inclination" (Babylonian Talmud Abodah Zarah 5b). "He who controls his evil disposition is mighty" (Abot 4:1). "Happy is he who repents while he is still a man. Happy is he who overrules his inclination

like a man" (Babylonian Talmud Abodah Zarah 19a).
"Let man seek to suppress the evil inclination by
means of the good" (Babylonian Talmud Berakhot
5b). "Let a man never say: 'I am a sinner and have
committed too many sins! What does it avail me
now to keep the commandments?' But if he has
committed many sins, let him the more zealously perform his duties." (Midrash le 'Olam 6)

That man has a free will in moral matters implies
not only that he possesses freedom of choice, the
ability to choose between good and evil. It implies
also that he is able to do what the commandments
require. The ethical action is within man's power
to perform. He can both will and do what is right.
In other words, throughout there is the theoretical
possibility that a man can completely fulfill the obligations of the Moral Law. Neither anything in the
thing itself, nor in man's own nature, nor in God's
determination, places any obstacle in the way of
man's performing what is a moral duty, a divine
command.

Is Christianity
Deterministic?

Let it be noted — and this is of fundamental importance to the question of the antithesis between
Pharisaic and primitive Christian ethics — that
neither Jesus nor the apostles meant that man did

not possess the possibility of choice in the line of conduct, or that it is impossible to perform fully all the actions which one makes up his mind to accomplish within the framework of a moral system. The view of primitive Christianity is not deterministic in the usual philosophical sense, so that man's actions are fully determined. Man is capable of choosing between different actions. He also possesses the ability to do outwardly what he has resolved to do. Therefore Jesus raises no objection when the rich young man declares that he has kept the commandments from his youth. On the contrary, His reply indicates that He approves of what the young man said: "One thing thou lackest" (Mark 10:21; Matt. 19:21; Luke 18:22). *Nor do we find anything in Paul's letters to indicate that he had not been able during the time he was a Pharisee to do all that the divine Law required.**

It goes without saying that there are people who find they are too weak to perform what they have resolved to do. But these are not the ones who here constitute the problem. They are reckoned in the category of "sinners." However, what at this point constitutes the decisive difference between the Phari-

---

*The author perhaps has in mind Luther's distinction between "doing the Law" and "fulfilling the Law." By "doing the Law" Luther meant outward conformity to the Law, without regard to one's heart-attitude toward God. "Fulfilling the Law" is possible only through the work of the Holy Spirit within man which leads him to serve God with delight and out of love, as if there were no Law. — Translator's note.

saic and the Christian view is that the Pharisee believes that man has the freedom to choose *between good and evil,* between doing the will of God and acting contrary to it, and that man is capable of performing the good he has resolved to do; *the Christian view,* is again that man in his natural state has the freedom to choose between different ways of conduct, and that he also has the ability to perform the deeds that he has chosen to do; *but he cannot choose what is good, and whatever ways of conduct he may choose, he can never produce what is good,* that is, so long as he remains "the old man." If a man therefore wills what is good, he must — as long as he has not become a new creation, received a new life — in reality turn his will toward that which is evil. Thus we plainly see how Paul can declare: "What I would, that do I not; but what I hate, that I do" (Rom. 7:15). And this is the actual background of Paul's description of the Jews quoted above (Rom. 2:17 to 24). The discovery made by the Christian, one who has become a new creature, is that what he believed to be good was in reality evil. For in the old relationship the concentration of the will can only accomplish this.

From the Christian point of view, the Pharisee, that is, the righteous, cannot get out of his way of thinking, his world. Consequently, if he determines to do the works of God, he is not on that account lifted out of his former way of thinking and transported to the divine world; but he remains with

his works in the world of the devil. The willpower
and energy which the righteous supposes is aimed at
doing good must of necessity be in the interest of
the evil, the satanic. Consequently, he will of necessity do the works of the devil, as Jesus declares.

To the Pharisaic way of thinking, however, such
a view is blasphemy against God and an affront to
all good men and all goodwill in the world. This
point of view, which is distinctive of Christianity,
may, however, have sprung from a deeper insight
into human nature than the Pharisaic insight, which
quite naturally appears to a Pharisaic age as the most
attractive and as the only reasonable one.

Meanwhile attention should also be called to the
other side of the matter — that a Christianity which
no longer has any understanding of the fact that man
such as he is can neither will nor do what is good,
nor is capable of discerning the voice of God — that
such a Christianity has already become Pharisaic and
has ceased to be Christianity. For with this principle
is bound up everything which in a fundamental and
irreconcilable way distinguishes Pharisaism from
Christianity.

Pharisaism Condemns
Hypocrisy

In this connection, however, the objection might
on the other hand again be raised that what Jesus

censured in the Pharisees was not their theory or their ethical demands but their personal hypocrisy and insincerity. To this it should be replied that the Pharisee was assuredly not a conscious hypocrite. In the Pharisees there is not to be found any conscious contradiction between doctrine and life. The Pharisees consciously condemn hypocrisy as the basest sin.

To the Pharisaic teaching, hypocrisy *(hanuppa)* falls under the category of falsehood, lying, comprising all manner of simulation, including such as pass under the name of polite behavior and courtesy. It is self-evident that religious or moral hypocrisy — pretense — must appear as particularly odious.

"Every man in whom is flattery brings wrath upon the world. Not only that, but his prayer remains unheard" (Babylonian Talmud Sotah 41b). "Any community in which is flattery is as repulsive as a menstruant woman" (Babylonian Talmud Sotah 42a). "Flatterers shall not come into the presence of God" (Ibid.). "Three the Holy One hates: he who speaks one thing with his mouth and another thing in his heart; he who possesses evidence concerning his neighbor and does not testify for him; and he who sees something indecent in his neighbor and testifies against him alone" (Babylonian Talmud Pesahim 113b). "Hypocrites must be unmasked, for they bring dishonor upon the name of God" (Tos. Yoma 5:12). "God has created all things except lies and falsehoods. These have been invented by men" (Pesikta Rabbati 24). The religious hypocrite is described thus: "Men believe him to be learned in the Scriptures, and he is not; they suppose that he knows the most ancient statutes, and he does not; he clothes himself in his mantle and his prayer ribbons — and to him the words apply: 'Those who are oppressed (by him) weep, and there is no one to comfort them.' But God says: 'It is incumbent upon Me to punish such'" (Ecclesiastes Rabbah 4:1). The hypocrite is also called "one whose inside is not like his outside" *(šä' en tóko k^e bāro)*. Such a one, according to Gamaliel II, was not worthy to pursue studies (Babylonian Talmud Berakhot 28b.) "Four kinds of people will not appear before the presence of God *(shekinah)*: scoffers *(lēsim)*, liars *(šakrānim)*, hypocrites *(h^{a}nēfim)*, and slanderers *(m^e sapp^e re l^e šon hārā')*." (Babylonian Talmud Sanhedrin 103a; Sotah 42a)

It cannot be sufficiently emphasized that the Pharisees also in practice — considered as a class and as a group, in other words, in the degree in which they were actually Pharisees — were by no means conscious hypocrites. With their keen eye for man's weaknesses and inclinations, they paid very close attention to themselves in this respect. It would be difficult to find a religious group which was so free from hypocrisy — in the sense in which this word is generally applied and understood in recent times — as were the Pharisees. As already emphasized, the Pharisees applied themselves most earnestly to their ethical and religious endeavors.

It was precisely this earnestness and this intensity which from the beginning brought into being the Pharisaic brotherhood and which characterized it throughout. Thus, one of the most unjust accusations that can be directed against the Pharisees is that they are hypocrites — that is, in the sense in which the word is now understood. No Christian in modern times can boast of such zeal in his religious and moral aspirations as that commonly displayed by the Pharisees.

Nevertheless the personal attitude which characterizes the Pharisee must, from the point of view of primitive Christianity, appear as hypocrisy. It might be expressed in this way: Pharisaic ethics must of necessity lead to *an actual, although of necessity also an unconscious, hypocrisy.* For what does a man do who, although he belongs to *one* environment in life, attempts to act as if he belonged to another environment? He attempts to be something which he is not, and never can be, so long as he remains what he is. He plays the part of someone else than he is. A hypocrite *(hypokrites)* in the New Testament really also means, as we know, an actor, one who seeks to accustom himself to something he himself is not. Now, an actor can certainly to some extent enter into another intellectual life and in this way at least reproduce, and for a brief time even be, what constitutes his role. However, there are limits beyond which he cannot go. Even as a person who does not experience love cannot with his perception comprehend what love is, even so a person who belongs to the world apart from God cannot receive the things of the Spirit of God. The more divine he seeks to be, the more intimately will he enter into alliance with the satanic, and will pray and labor for the advance-ment of the devil.

The Fundamental
Christian Conception

The fundamental Christian view, on the other hand, is that man can will to do good and obey the divine will only on the assumption that he has be-come a *new creature,* a new being, that he has moved from his former environment into a new en-vironment, that he has been born again by the Spirit. This has been made possible for men only because Christ came down into the world of humanity and wrought salvation which involves the deliverance of the human to the divine.

To the Pharisaic manner of thinking, this Chris-tian view is simply incomprehensible and appears as sheer folly. Therefore it is obvious that a man who follows the Pharisaic principle and undertakes to become righteous simply cannot recognize or ac-cept the Son of God as long as he continues to be righteous. *The "righteous" can therefore never be saved or redeemed as long as he is "righteous." He must first be brought back to the point of zero* and become a sinner.

The Christian view is expressed in the New Testament in the following manner: In the Logos (Christ) was life, and the Life was the Light of men. The Light was in the world, and the world comprehended it not. He came unto His own, and His own received Him not. But as many as received Him, to them gave He power to become the sons of God, which were born, not of blood, nor of the will of the flesh, nor of the will of man, but of God. For truly, he who has not been born again cannot see the kingdom of God. (John 1:1-13)

By way of antithesis, the Pharisaic way of looking at the matter is as follows:

> In the moral action man becomes conscious of the ability which dwells within him; by virtue of this ability he can and must make a decision, and therein he experiences his freedom. Good and evil are placed before him in order that he may make a choice. Human life is not a matter of fate, but is dependent upon the decision which man himself makes. The goal is provided for him to which his freedom leads him. If he should turn away from God, he has the ability to turn around in order to walk the way upon which he will find God. He is capable of making good what he has done amiss; he is able to cleanse himself. His deeds — his good deeds — are what bring about the reconciliation. This is accomplished not by a miracle, nor by any sacrament, but by the freedom implanted in him.

And through the reconciliation man finds the
new freedom and thereby the new responsibility; the reconciliation becomes the way, the
new purpose." (Leo Baeck)

The Doctrine of Pharisaism
Concerning Freedom

Man's freedom is a much discussed subject in
the writings of Pharisaism, that is, the rabbinical
writings. The word "freedom" is used mainly in
two connections. (1) It is sometimes used in the
sense that man's will — as already pointed out above
— is always free; he has the freedom to choose between good and evil (formal freedom). (2) Sometimes the concept of freedom is used in connection
with the Law. The Jew becomes a free man by
virtue of possessing the Law or the "precepts" (material freedom).

For him the Law (or the precept: *Torah*) is the
"law of liberty" (cf. James 1:25), that which guarantees him his freedom. For God has created man
to be free. If by his free choice he chooses sin and
does what is evil, then, to be sure, he will for a time
be a slave of sin. But he has the capacity to decide
for God. And in the Law, in the *Torah*, he has been
given the rules according to which he can act in
order that as an upright and God-fearing person he
may be a free man.

We have already referred to the view of Pharisaism in regard to freedom of the will, namely, that, with respect to morality, man possesses perfect freedom of will, which implies that he himself has the capacity of choosing between good and evil, that he has the ability to do what is good, and that he is able to fulfill the moral obligation in every detail and in every moment of life — in other words, to be "perfectly righteous" *(sadikk gāmur)*, which is the technical expression for this. This human freedom in moral matters is grounded in the will of God. That man is able to do what is good is contingent upon the fact that God has given him this freedom of choice. That man can actually fulfill all the requirements of the Moral Law — that is, the Law of God — is for Pharisaism a logical conclusion of the fact that God has given man freedom of will with the intention that there might thereby arise men who of their own free will did what is good, that is, what God wills. And since God wills that the good should be brought to perfection in the world, it is unthinkable that He would place obstacles in the way of the good being achieved. Accordingly, He cannot make it impossible for the person who has resolved to do good to carry out his resolve. And no one but God determines what is possible and what is impossible in this world. In other words, it is possible for man assiduously to perform his duty, zealously to accomplish the will of God.

It is by no means only the perfectly righteous who are free according to Pharisaic view. One is already free by virtue of possessing the Law, by one's knowledge of God's will, and by one's decision to do what is good. One thereby attains to what is properly called freedom in Pharisaic terminology. For the terms "free" and "freedom" are used less frequently in connection with what we call freedom of will or freedom of choice. There one uses the words "able," "ability," "power," and the like. In Pharisaic usage the words "free" and "freedom" pertain to the Law of God, to the matter of belonging to God, to a special relationship to God. The Pharisees frequently speak of "taking upon themselves the yoke of the kingdom of heaven" (compare the expression in Matt. 11:29), meaning thereby the decision to obey God's Law, to perform the ethical duties, and particularly to confess God as the true Sovereign and King of the world. This implies that one is placed directly under God's rule, that man has as his king the King of the whole world. And to the Pharisee this logically becomes the true "freedom." He who has assumed the yoke of the kingdom of heaven is thereby released from every other yoke and placed directly under God. The yoke of the kingdom of God, then, cannot be construed as a burden; for the Pharisee this is actually what Jesus says about His yoke in the Matthew passage alluded to: "My yoke is easy, and My burden is light." To the Pharisee the yoke of the kingdom of God was a source of joy and freedom. When one had God as his King, one was happy and had an experience of being free.

This freedom, then, is by no means freedom from obligations, freedom to do just anything. But freedom is a freedom in the strength of one's own decision — as a mature man or as a son in the home — to do what God, the Father, wills. By the very act of taking upon himself the yoke of the kingdom of heaven one became a self-determining instrument in God's hand who of his own volition participated in God's government of the world, in the realization of the divine world plan.

It is therefore quite natural that freedom is often synonymous with being free-born, nobility, a privileged position. "Him who takes upon himself the yoke of the *Torah* God releases from all other yokes, such as that imposed by secular governments and worldly occupation" (Abot 3:6). "He who takes upon himself the yoke of the *Torah* is released from loyalty to earthly kingdoms" *(Tanchuma, we-zoth hab-be-raka)*. Freedom under the dominion of God is freedom from all other dominion, but also, through perfect obedience to God, participation in His rule. For God's will alone shall hold sway in the world. He who perceives it as his duty to act perfectly in accordance with the will of God sees as a consequence thereof that it is his duty to permit the will of God to prevail in the world. However, since he knows his own will to be identical with God's will, he must also recognize that the only proper thing is *that the content of his own will determines what happens in the world.*"

When this ideal condition does not correspond to the reality of the present, it is thought of in every case as being reserved for the future in which perfection shall have begun. This future is called the coming age, the world to come. A Pharisee can thus ask the question and reply as follows: "What is meant by this statement of Job: 'The small and the great are there; and the servant is free from his master'? (Job 3:19). It means that he who humbles himself for the sake of the *Torah* in this world is magnified in the next; and he who makes himself a servant to the (study of the) *Torah* in this world becomes free in the next." (Babylonian Talmud Baba Metzia 85b)

Thus we may summarize the Pharisaic concept of freedom as follows: Man has at all times the freedom to choose between good and evil; he can decide to do the one or the other; he who determines to do good — or which is the same thing — to do the will of God, has thereby become a free individual who occupies a privileged position. He is free from the mastery of all other powers and from their claim to his obedience; he is directly subject to God. By his own self-determination he is the voluntary instrument for the realization of God's will in the world, for the realization of God's plan for the world.

The Christian Conception of Freedom and the Consequences of the Pharisaical Conception

Here we again encounter a fundamental difference between Pharisaic opinion and Christian conviction. Probably no one has experienced, known, and constantly proclaimed this difference as pointedly as has Paul, who himself had been a Pharisee. According to the Christian view, the person who remains in the old environment has no freedom of choice whatever between good and evil. He is and remains a slave to sin. The corrupt tree is and remains a corrupt tree and can only bring forth corrupt fruit. Therefore the Law is not a law of freedom but of bondage. The Law is not a rule according to which man can act, but an indictment showing him how he ought to have acted but did not act. The Law cannot make anyone free or alive, but it came into being because of sin (Gal. 3:19 ff.). The Law reveals the absolute corruption of the righteous man, showing that he is worse than sin itself, as Paul interprets it in Romans 2.

Therefore the Christianity disguised in Pharisaic garb represented by Erasmus was completely repulsive to the genuine Christianity which Luther presented in his *De servo arbitrio*. The law of liberty, which to the Pharisaic way of thinking appears so natural and reasonable, actually leads to its expressing itself in human pretensions, in claims to human coercion and ultimately to absolute domination.

Actually, Pharisaic Judaism has consistently advanced such claims. Because the rabbis are convinced that their principles express the divine will, they have advocated as their ultimate requirement that the whole world shall be subject to these principles and be judged by their representatives. The claim to domination and to judgment is the natural consequence of the idea of the law of freedom. The society which bases obedience to the divine will upon man's free will ends by claiming world domination. For Pharisaism therefore it becomes self-evident and logically necessary that God's supremacy must imply a claim to ultimate ascendancy in *this* world. This constitutes the background for the sharp and seemingly unjust words which Jesus, according to John, addressed to the Pharisees: "Ye are of this world; I am not of this world. . . . Ye judge after the flesh; I judge no man. . . . Ye are of your father the devil, and the lusts of your father ye will do." (John 8:23, 15, 44)

*The Teaching of Pharisaism Concerning
the Divine Spark in Man (nešama) and the Fall.
The Good and the Evil Disposition*

Most intimately bound up with the Pharisaic teaching concerning the freedom of the will and the freeborn state of him who is obedient to God is the idea of the indestructible divine soul, the innermost and vital part of man. In the liturgy of the daily morning worship in the synagog there appears a well-known prayer, the so-called *Elohai Nešāmā,* which begins with the words: "My God, the soul *(nešāmā)* which Thou hast given me is pure." This *nešāmā* is conceived as a divine vestige in man, a spark preexistent and eternal.

Inasmuch as this *nešāmā,* according to the view of Pharisaism, is indestructible, Pharisaic Judaism is unable to comprehend the fall of man and even less the idea of original sin. The story of the Fall in Genesis is therefore regarded by the Pharisaic teachers merely as a typical example of the disobedience against God of which man under certain circumstances is guilty. They speak of the evil impulses in man, which oppose the good impulses during his earthly sojourn. These evil impulses, however, are able only for a time to obscure the purity of the soul, the divine spark in man, but they can never extinguish it. As soon as man, whose own fault it is that this spark is obscured, again turns about and takes the right path, *nešāmā* stands at his disposal. From this point of view man's task may be defined as seeking to bring everything within himself into harmony with his noblest part, with his *nešāmā,* and placing his whole being under the dominion of the divine spark and thereby becoming free. Having done this, he has fulfilled the destiny which God intended for him.

Elohai Nešāmā, the prayer referred to above,

contains the following: "My God, the soul which
Thou hast placed in me is pure. Thou hast fashioned
it in me, Thou didst breathe it into me, and Thou
preservest it within me, and Thou wilt one day take
it from me and restore it to me in the time to come.
So long as the soul is within me I give thanks unto
Thee, O Lord, my God, and the God of my fathers,
Sovereign of all worlds, Lord of all souls. Blessed
art Thou, O Lord, who restorest souls to dead
corpses." This prayer, which is included in the
ritual of the daily morning worship in the synagog,
is quoted in the *Babylonian Talmud* (Berakhot 60b)
as the prayer which the individual is to pray every
morning immediately upon awakening. The teaching which it contains, then, is something that is
most solemnly impressed upon the mind of the
pious Pharisee. Accordingly, here it is not a question of an isolated pronouncement of some individual scribe but of a fundamental principle of Pharisaism. This principle also finds expression in other
connections. In the *Babylonian Talmud* (Shab-
bat 152b) we read: "Return the spirit to God as
He gave it to thee." The indestructible spirit re-
turns to its Source.

From this fundamental view, however, Pharisaism by no means draws the conclusion that man's
imperfections and sins stem from the body in which
the soul is confined during this earthly life. On the
contrary, the body is also created by God for the
service of the soul, and in its structure it is perfect

and has nothing to do with moral merit or guilt, virtue or defect. Man's sin is the result of his own free choice, and is not due to any disposition in him or any part of him, whether it be his soul or his body. Consequently Gaon Saadja in *Emunot we Deot* can declare: "In all of man (as he is created) there is nothing unclean. He is pure." Man is created in the image of God.

The Good and Evil Disposition:
jésär tov *and* jésär hārā'

On the other hand, one can say that man is accompanied by two forces which separately seek to influence him and to determine his choice and his conduct. They are called "the good disposition" and "the evil disposition," *jésär tov* and *jésär hārā'*. These are deeply considered as moral functions designed by God for man's constant testing and training. Only exceptionally and figuratively can the evil disposition be represented as an evil power, on an equality with Satan.

When the creation story, Gen. 1:31, declares: "and behold, it was very good," the "and" indicates that both the evil and the good disposition are meant. "Is the evil disposition 'very good'? Yes, if the evil disposition were not present, no one would build a house or take a wife, beget children or do business. This is what Solomon means when he declares (Eccl. 4:4): 'I considered all travail, and every right work, that for this man is envied of his neighbor'" (Genesis Rabbah 9:7; Ecclesiastes Rabbah 3:11; Jalkut Genesis, No. 16). The meaning is that the evil disposition is included in "all that God had done," concerning which it is said that "it was very good." The evil inclination has as its purpose to exercise and strengthen man's power of resistance, so that his determination to do good will be motivated by actual moral strength. But then the good disposition — as in the quotation referred to — may be thought of as being the direct motive power for the performance of useful and necessary things.

"God said: 'I have created the evil inclination; be on your guard lest it seduce you to sin! But if it has enticed you to sin, then see that you turn about! Then I will take away your sin.' This is the significance of the statement: 'I have made' — namely, the evil inclination — 'I will bear' — namely, sin — 'I will carry, and will deliver' — namely, from judgment (Is. 46:4)." (Midrash Tillim 32:4)

Man's task is to make the good inclination the master over the evil inclination. When Prov. 24:21 declares: "My son, fear thou the Lord and the king," it rather means: "make the good inclination king over the evil inclination, which is also called a king." (Numbers Rabbah 15:14; Ecclesiastes Rabbah 9:14)

The evil disposition may, through man's own fault — by following its tempting directions — be-

come the master over man's body. The following
parable illustrates the difference between the Pharisaic idea and the view which regards the body as
a natural prison of the spirit and an impediment to
the spirit's activity:

> When man yields, allowing the evil impulse to
> lead him into unchastity, all parts of man's body
> become the willing servants of the evil impulse;
> the evil inclination then becomes king over the
> body's 248 parts. If man later undertakes to fulfill a commandment, all his members are sluggish, since the evil impulse is king over his 248
> parts. The good inclination resembles a prisoner who lies shackled in prison, as it is written:
> "Out of prison he cometh to reign" (Eccl. 4:14).
> "This refers to the good impulse which is like
> a slave within man, who yielded to the evil impulse, but who leaves the prison to assume the
> mastery when man is transformed and resolves
> to do what is right and good." (Abot de Rabbi
> Nathan, Ch. 16)

That man is able to overcome the evil inclination
and to perform the good when he wants to, does
not, however, mean, according to Pharisaism, that
he has this ability *of himself,* but he is dependent
on God's willingness to assist him when he directs
his will toward that which is good. A certain prayer,
for example, goes as follows: "It is manifest and
open to Thee, O Lord, my God and the God of my
fathers, that we have no strength to resist the evil
disposition. Therefore may it please Thee, Lord,

to strike it down and suppress it in order that we may do Thy will with all our heart according to our will." (Palestinian Talmud Berakhot IV: 2, 29b, 60)

It is entirely natural, then, for a Jewish scholar to characterize Judaism's view of sin in the following manner: "Judaism does not contain any myth of sin which is a myth of fate, for its prophets destroyed the rudiments of such a myth. Judaism knows nothing of original sin, that event in which man as mere object suffers its effects. For Judaism sin is the fate prepared by the individual when he disowns himself and makes of himself a mere object. Man does not fall into the sin of his fate, but into the fate of his sin." (Leo Baeck, *The Essence of Judaism,* Schocken Books [New York, 1948], pp. 161, 162.) "Judaism rejects original sin as well as the idea of the unclean corporeality. The words of Eccl. 7:29, 'God hath made man upright; but they have sought out many inventions,' are explained as follows in *Midrash Jelammedenu:* 'God, the just and upright, created man in His image in order that in his striving after righteousness he might display Godlikeness. But in their discord and in their divided mind men have obscured this Godlikeness.'" (Kaufmann Kohler, *Grundriss einer systematischen Theologie des Judentums,* p. 162)

> Even Judaism has concerned itself with the story of the disobedience of which Adam, the first man, was guilty. But of an original sin which after that time could no longer be over-

come, or even that death should from now on
be appointed for all men as a punishment for
sin, of this there is not the remotest reference
in Judaism. Judaism makes no more of this
narrative than what it purports to be. It does
not seek in this narrative, nor does it conclude
from it, a solution of the enigma of man's nature. It ascribes to man, before as well as after
Adam's fall, the ability of his own free choice
to undertake and to perform what is good; in
fact, it obligates him to do so. It likewise rec-
ognizes in the sensually disposed man the exist-
ing tendency to sin, but nevertheless insists that
he has the ability to subdue this tendency and
that he has the power to eradicate the sin which
he has committed and to compensate for it by
personal penitence. Judaism, then, is not without a doctrine of salvation: man finds salvation
from sin through his own conversion and the
grace of God (Ps. 130:7, 8). (Abraham Loe-
wenthal LJI)

*Christian Ethics and the Doctrine
of the Fall*

The fundamental difference between Pharisaism
and Christianity at this point appears very clearly
in Paul, the former Pharisee, when he writes: "By
one man sin entered into the world, and death by
sin; and so death passed upon all men, for that all
have sinned. . . . For the judgment was by one to
condemnation. . . . For . . . by one man's offense
death reigned by one." (Rom. 5:12, 16, 17)

According to the Christian view the divine life in man has not only been obscured; it has been totally lost. Men wander about in darkness, possessing no ability in themselves to find the divine light. Therefore, according to the Christian point of view, there can be no such thing as an indestructible spirit in man, no *nešāmā,* or a spirit which guarantees a state of belonging together with God. For this reason man cannot through his spirit ascertain his destination. One might unconditionally express the Christian view of man by saying that man possesses no spirit whatever. The regenerate man, however, possesses a spirit, the Spirit of Christ. In him dwells the Spirit of God, which was given to him by redemption. But it was necessary for the Savior to come into the world to mediate the divine Spirit to man. Thus man has truly attained his own free life; but he is not capable of finding it by himself. By reading 1 Corinthians 2 in its context, one can reach no other conclusion than that Paul completely denies that the unsaved person has any spirit. "But the natural man," he declares, "receiveth not the things of the Spirit of God; for they are foolishness unto him; neither can he know them, because they are spiritually discerned. But he that is spiritual judgeth all things, yet he himself is judged of no man. For who hath known the mind of the Lord, that he may instruct Him? But we have the mind of Christ." (1 Cor. 2:14-16)

The Ability to Judge
What Is Right

The difference expressed in these words of Paul leads to a significant consequence. The Pharisaic view of man's natural endowment of a divine, indestructible spiritual vestige has as its consequence the thought that man is capable of discerning and comprehending the divine commandments and the divine will. In other words, man is said to have the ability rightly to judge and discern the divine. To be sure, the Pharisaic theory does not demand of every man that he be able independently to judge and to determine this will or that moral duty. On the contrary, the doctrine has to form an unbroken chain of traditions from the first day when the law was revealed to the present promulgators of the doctrine. But in reality one is convinced that the correct interpretation of the Law is given to man by his saying yes to the Law, that is, to the moral commandments. And to say yes to the Law is tantamount to placing one's life under the guidance of the divine spark. The person who has said yes to the Law of course knows and is capable of judging what God wills.

But now, if Christianity is right in its teaching that man does not have a spirit whose origin is from God, that he does not have a divine vestige but only a psyche (soul) which belongs entirely to the context of the world which is alien to God, it follows that the "righteous" as a rule for his moral conduct, for his conduct which is directed toward obedience to God, uses something which of necessity must lead to the very opposite. *A person who wants to do what is right must constantly do what is wrong; and inversely, what is said to be right will to him appear as foolishness, erroneous, or evil; and therefore he will brusquely reject it.* He will be blinded, and having eyes, he will not be able to see; and having ears, he will not be able to hear. The gospels are replete with graphic examples of such conduct on the part of the Pharisees.

The Hypocritical Example

Already in the Sermon on the Mount, in Matthew 6, attention is called whereto the Pharisaic principles could and must lead. The Pharisee can by no means admit that he practices righteousness in order to be seen by others. This is contrary to Pharisaic principles and is expressly condemned. "A man who gives charity in secret is greater than Moses, our teacher, for of Moses it is written: 'I was afraid of the anger and hot displeasure' (Deut. 9:19); but of him who gives charity secretly it is written: 'A gift in secret pacifieth anger' (Prov. 21:14)" (Babylonian Talmud Baba Batra 9b). "He who gives alms to a poor person publicly, falls under the judgment of God" (Babylonian Talmud Chagiga 5a). Moreover, even from the Phari-

saic viewpoint, according to the common principle
that "the good must be done for its own sake," it
is actually condemned to practice righteousness in
order to be seen of men. "Every commandment
that a man fulfills in this world which is not done
out of love and the fear of God is done in vain."
(Rabbi Akiba's Alphabeth, the letter *gimel*)

From the point of departure of primitive Christianity, he who is righteous without having become
"a new creature" or entered into the new life, must,
however, of necessity be led to practice righteousness in the presence of men in order to be seen by
them, even though essentially he does not desire
this and condemns such an attitude. For he cannot reckon with circumstances other than those
which he understands, and these have reference
only to the external. He himself wants to do what
is right, and he will also be able to lead others to
do what is right. However, he cannot conceive of
this as being accomplished in any other way than
through the fact that, not only by his testimony but
also by his own life, he is showing others what is
right and pleasing in the sight of God. Therefore
he cannot escape being an example, and he must
be a good example for others; and the natural result of this striving to be an example is hypocrisy.
The concern to be a good example will necessarily
cause one's attention to be focused upon what men
will say, upon how they will construe and judge
one's actions. And this will be a matter of constant

concern. For it is important that one should be an example, not only on certain occasions but in all of one's actions and conduct.

And this example must be of such a nature as to win men's approval. An example that fails to win men's approval has no molding influence. The honest and upright person's actions and conduct must be such as to elicit the praise of men. The result is that one soon reaches the point where one is constantly, in all circumstances and in all of one's actions, seeking men's approval.

This also has other consequences. Actions and conduct which in themselves are proper — those, in other words, for which the acting person can answer before God and his own conscience — but which provoke the disapproval of men always become questionable. The person who directs his energies in this way soon reaches the point where he refrains from doing what he himself judges to be the only right thing, if this should evoke general disapproval. However, the righteous or the upright, who is convinced that his point of departure is right, that his striving is honest, and who is persuaded that he is on the right path, is powerless to change his mind, and in most instances he is also incapable of discerning that he is acting as he does. It is this moral deterioration in the morally excellent person that may be alluded to in the Sermon on the Mount, in Matt. 6:1-18, with these introductory words: "Take heed that ye do not your righteousness before men, to be seen of them; otherwise ye have no reward of your Father which is in heaven" (Revised Version).

It is obvious that the development in the direction of a righteousness which is done to be seen — an unconscious hypocrisy — which we have here described, must lead to another important attitude on the part of the one who develops in this direction. By being constantly awake to the opinion of men, and viewing this action in its external relation, he will again and again neglect every opportunity for spontaneous action out of a truly good heart. Moreover, experience teaches that the righteous, the moralist, even though he may bear the Christian name and regard himself as an earnest and zealous Christian, is utterly without feeling. The immediate warmheartedness will necessarily be more and more rarely seen in him. And as a natural result, he does not act out of a deeper self-examination in the presence of God. For him God will actually fade more and more into the background, even though he may have God's name upon his lips. That this development is equally possible for the Christian as for the Jew is obvious. But whoever it may be that drifts into such a development, he is definitely not a good man, and that precisely because he aims to be an "example." This is Pharisaism.

A truly good man, on the other hand, may in externals so conduct himself that his manner of life will necessarily be censured by those who have the

Pharisaic mind. Thus Jesus' conduct and manner of life were severely criticized by the Pharisees. "Behold a man gluttonous and a winebibber, a friend of publicans and sinners" (Matt. 11:19; Luke 7:34). The Christian, however, does what he does, not because he finds it proper and expedient but because he cannot do otherwise; and yet it will always be evident later that he did what was right insofar as he permitted himself to be led by the Spirit of Christ and lives in the Spirit of Christ.

Therefore Paul, who declares that the natural man is incapable of discerning God and His will, and thereby, of course, what is right (1 Cor. 2: 14-16), can declare that he who is transformed so that he receives the new life is able to "prove what is that good and acceptable and perfect will of God." (Rom. 12:2)

The question might, however, be raised as to whether there actually is a fundamental difference between Pharisaic and Christian morality, so that if Pharisaic ethics were applied, it would lead to the consequences referred to, while if Christian ethics were applied, it would lead to the opposite consequences. To this we may reply that it is here principally a matter of making clear what constituted the decisive antithesis between Jesus and primitive Christianity on the one hand and Pharisaism on the other hand. And in that case we must point out that Jesus sees such a danger as being inherent in Pharisaism and judges this danger as being extremely serious. It should be said that we are concerned here with the Pharisaic *principle* which Jesus condemns in His opponents and of which He warns His disciples. However, it is therefore quite possible that the Pharisaic principle did not in the case of all Pharisees lead to the development which Jesus censured. They may have been better in practice than in their theory, just as Christians may be Pharisees in practice. Indeed, the Pharisaic principle is a danger which is a constant threat to the Christian life.

As regards the development of the concept of righteousness which may be called the hypocrisy of being motivated by the desire to be an example — that is, the hypocrisy which results from the striving to be an example — the question may be anticipated: Did Jesus consistently hold to the view which forms the basis of the first half of Matthew 6? Do we not also have other utterances that point in another direction? And are there not in primitive Christian writings certain statements by the leaders in primitive Christianity which modify this view? We might then conclusively cite the words of Jesus in which He speaks of the disciples as the light of the world: "Ye are the light of the world. A city that is set on an hill cannot be hid. Neither do men light a candle and put it under a bushel, but on a candlestick; and it giveth light unto all that are in the house. Let your light so shine before men that they may see your good works and glorify your Father which is in heaven" (Matt. 5:14-16). Does not this sound like an exhortation to display one's works before others? It might likewise be asked whether the words of Jesus concerning offending a little one, and the curse resting upon such an offense, do not point to the destructive influence of the poor example (Matt. 18:6). And from the side of the leaders of primitive Christianity one might recall such statements as Paul's exhortation that the strong should take into consideration the conscience of the weak. This would also be said to imply that the Christian or the upright person must consider the effect of his actions upon others, so that even though what he does may be right in the sight of God and his own conscience, it might nevertheless be harmful, since it may have a detrimental effect upon the observer who has a different type of conscience. In other words, we would be reasoning like the Pharisees.

Christians as the Light of the World

As regards the words of the Sermon on the Mount concerning the disciples as the light of the world, this in reality belongs in a context which is the very opposite of that in which the hypocritical example belongs. In order to understand this, it is also necessary to understand the wholly different appraisement which applies in this context. This appraisement can perhaps to some extent be illustrated by an example from daily life. Let us suppose that as a judge we have an ordinary natural man who makes no claim to being especially righteous or perfect, nor to being better than people in general. If this man is brought into the presence of one who is a strict moralist, who acts according to rigid principles, and who is an "example for others," it is quite possible that the ordinary man experiences a feeling of admiration in the presence of this example.

Contributing to this is, of course, the upbringing which the ordinary man has received, which has emphasized that certain matters are sinful and that that person is better who can entirely refrain from these things and who sees to it that others who do not refrain are informed that they are corrupt. The ordinary man admires the exemplary man — or in the language of the New Testament, the "righteous man" — for his moral strength. At times it may happen that the ordinary man wishes that he might be like this example. But what the ordinary man in no circumstances can think of doing is to praise God for the deeds of the exemplary man or for the fact that there are such model men. The exemplary man inspires respect and probably fear — for in most cases he is stern and inconsiderate with the severity and inconsiderateness which accompanies one who believes that he acts in the Spirit of God and does God's bidding — *but no one re-*

joices in the fact that the exemplary man is to be found or because of what he does. The life of the "righteous" does not direct one's glance upward toward anything higher; it does not provoke one's thought to anything which exalts or inspires, to anything which belongs to a more beautiful and a more lovely world. On the contrary, it frequently happens that the "righteous" man arouses resentment, driving the ordinary man into the power of evil. It is evident that such a person, who is here called "exemplary" or "righteous," is supposedly one who practices his righteousness in order to be seen by men; but it is equally evident that he is not God's light in the world for which men glorify the heavenly Father. Thus the words of Jesus concerning His disciples as the light of the world can have no connection with such a person; and thereby it is likewise clear that this statement of Jesus does not imply an exhortation to practice one's righteousness before men, as the exemplary righteous do.

He who is the "light" of the world is frequently one whom men do not regard as a righteous person, perhaps mainly because he is in no wise recognized by the righteous as being a true representative of their spiritual family, but on the contrary is regarded as very imperfect. There is, however, something about him or her which causes the ordinary man to feel edified, happy, and strengthened by observing this man or woman. Even though one would seldom feel that one could ascribe to him

or her the epithet "a righteous" or "pious" person
or a "true Christian" — and such a person would by
no means ascribe this epithet to himself — yet the
very life of this person directs one's thoughts to
God, leading the observer to become aware of the
fact, and to realize, that there is still something
good and holy and exalted in life. However, everyone who observes this person is certain that he himself has no idea of the good works that he does and
that he himself makes no effort to "make a display
of his light." Least of all would he wish to be regarded as an example or desire that others would
conduct themselves as he does. *In order to "let
one's light shine before men" according to the words
of Jesus, it is necessary, then, that even the remotest
thought that one is worthy of being an example, or
by one's conduct to make a favorable impression on
others, must be completely alien.* In order to let
one's light shine, one must first be a light; and to
be a light obviously means in this connection to be
ignited by the divine Light. However, he who is
ignited by the divine Light is himself entirely con-
sumed and is unable of himself to shine, even if
this were perfect obedience to the will of God.

The Offense

From the insight into this context it likewise
becomes plain that the statement of Jesus regard-

ing the offense does not imply any support for the attitude of the hypocritical example. For one need only recall that what Jesus denounces is the fact of the offense: "Woe to that man by whom the offense cometh!" (Matt. 18:7). Accordingly, one need only observe in what instance an offense can take place. It is granted that a poor example may seduce, just as an offense may take place by direct persuasion and studied effort. The latter falls under the badge of the satanic, the former under the ordinary "sin" category. However, he who, according to what was just cited, is to be represented as a light which causes one to think of the good in the world, cannot possibly cause offense. On the other hand, the "righteous," the strict moralist, the hypocritical example, may cause offense; that is to say, he may cause another to fall simply by the disgust which such a one arouses in another person with sound mind. The latter may then also come to abhor what the good "example" professes to represent, impelling him to do the very opposite of everything that the example does. To the righteous example may assuredly be applied the words of St. Paul in Rom. 2:24: "The name of God is blasphemed among the Gentiles through you." As stated, this righteous one himself is perhaps praised or at least admired, but he becomes an occasion for the blaspheming of Christ and Christianity, secretly or openly. If the hypocritical example has been an inspiration, he has been so only in a destructive direction, either by seducing others to become "whited sepulchres" like himself or, as was indicated a moment ago, by arousing the resentment of others, forcing them into the power of evil and vice.

Consideration for the Weak in Faith and Conscience

We come now to St. Paul's familiar exhortation to Christians to consider those who are "weak in the faith" (Rom. 14:1) or whose "conscience" is "weak," that is, sensitive. This has often been interpreted to mean that it is the Christian's duty not "to be an offense to anyone"; and not to be an offense to anyone is in turn interpreted to mean not to provoke another's disapproval. If such an interpretation of the words and the concept were correct, St. Paul would be made directly to exhort to what Jesus vigorously condemns. Christian morality would then consist essentially in seeking to avoid all conduct, every act and every word, which might evoke someone's disapproval. For one could not distinguish between the approval and disapproval of different persons and say that one had to have regard for some people's disapproval, but not for that of others. For this would mean that the instances when one did not take into consideration the disapproval of others would depend either upon the person, the position, and the relation of those

disapproving, or upon the importance of the disapproval which is voiced. In the former instance
it would be a question of taking into consideration
the person whose unchristian character requires no
proof. In the latter instance the statement about
considering the disapproval of others would nullify
itself, for it would then mean that one has regard
for a disapproval when the disapproval is legitimate
from the ethical point of view. And it could hardly
be legitimate except when the act which was disapproved was ethically reprehensible. And the sup-
position was precisely that the act would be ethically
defensible or positively meritorious, but that it
should be avoided for the sake of others. Consequently the statement, if it is to have any moral
significance at all, must, from this point of departure, mean that one is not permitted to do anything
that by itself is right, provided there are some who
disapprove of it, whatever might be the nature of
the disapproval.

If the objection is raised that St. Paul only meant
that one should take into consideration those who
are Christians — that is, those in the congregation
who were weak in faith and in conscience — such
an objection would only render the viewpoint still
more untenable. For the one who aims to be an
example must aim equally much to be an example
for those who are not Christians. If he is to consider those whose faith is weak, even though they
are Christians, he must even more so consider those

who must be said to be still weaker in faith, since they as yet have no faith at all, namely, the non-Christians. It must be just as important not to give non-Christians a false conception of Christianity by one's conduct as not to give those who are already Christians such a false conception. Such a principle issues in a truly sorry affair, a spineless attitude, which, if it were the attitude of Christianity, would compel one to the value judgment that Christian morality is the most miserable of all conceivable moralities.

It must, however, be pointed out that St. Paul himself by no means applied such a principle. On the contrary, Gal. 2:11-14 he rebukes the apostle Peter because in a certain degree he appears to have acted according to such a principle. According to the Swedish translation of the Bible, Paul judges Peter thus: "He had been found guilty of offense." What Peter had done and what Paul so severely condemns would, according to the interpretation which would here be assumed if Paul's words were to lend support to the "example principle," be nothing other than what Paul enjoins upon those to whom he writes in the First Epistle to the Corinthians and in the Epistle to the Romans. For Peter had first eaten together with the Gentiles in Antioch, but later, when the strictest Christians (those with "weaker conscience") came to Antioch from Jerusalem, Peter, intimated by them, drew back and

separated himself. This, that Peter did not partici-
pate in a feast when this was thought to give offense
to certain other brethren, is a manner of conduct
which Paul, according to this interpretation, would
recommend in his letters; however, at the same time
he most severely disapproved of this when he found
Peter doing it. This gives a powerful argument to
the suspicion that the current interpretation is not
correct.

Nor need one go farther than the word which
Paul utters in connection with the statement alluded
to in the Epistle to the Romans as well as in the
First Epistle to the Corinthians. For the current
interpretation and its application would imply that
others be given the right to rebuke someone for
a manner of conduct or a behavior which is unas-
sailable, according to the Christian view, and that
the one who is rebuked would then out of consideration for this reprimand change his conduct. However, in Rom. 14:3, 4 Paul expressly declares: "Let
not him that eateth despise him that eateth not;
and let not him which eateth not judge him that
eateth; for God hath received him. Who art thou
that judgest another man's servant? To his own
master he standeth or falleth. Yea, he shall be
holden up; for God is able to make him stand."
Here it is stated as plainly as it possibly can be that
*the one must not set himself up as a judge over
others in these matters;* and from this it follows
that the Christian *does not have to take into ac-*

count such judges — or their censure — as regard
themselves as capable of judging another Christian
for a manner of conduct which his Lord permits
him. What Paul speaks of, then, is not consideration for the people who judge, be they ever so exalted and conscientious Christians in their own esti-
mation, but rather *consideration for those who are
actually weak,* that is, *those who might be led away
from Christ by my conduct.* This is the sole norm.
To yield to the judgment of others is "hypocrisy"
(Gal. 2:13) and cowardice. The Christian must, on
the contrary, be prepared at all times to have the
"righteous" against himself; this belongs to the suf-
fering of Christ whose measure is never filled in
this life. (Phil. 3:10)

The General Perverseness
of the "Righteous"

In reality the hypocritical example is only one
characteristic of the general depravity, the per-
verseness, to which the principle leads which is
here presented as Pharisaical. The "old man," to
use Paul's words, when he would do good without
first becoming a new man, but supposes that he
simply becomes a new man by doing what is described as good, will, as already stated, of necessity,
as a result of the application of all good principles,
produce that which is perverted. He will pervert

the ethical principles, reversing them. In his hand they will serve the opposite end: evil.

When now the "righteous" person determines to do God's will, but is not first born again and awakened to a higher life, he cannot discern what is God's will. He is only firmly convinced that he now serves God and is a child of God. However, what he wills, no matter where he turns, cannot be anything but his own will or such desires, motives, impulses, and commands as are derived from the environment which belongs to his world. Since he now imagines that he is doing the will of God, the actual condition only becomes this: *he believes that his own desires and wishes are the will of God.* For example, he refrains from human arrogance, imagining that he is humble; but he retains his pride under the guise of the lofty demands of divine truth. Therefore we often observe that *he who talks much about his humility is extremely vain.* He refrains from all lust for power and revengefulness, but he has by no means abandoned the lust for power and revenge. Nor does he in reality become *less desirous of power and revenge,* but rather more so. *For now he can do so completely without regard for others in the name of God.* He imagines that when he now seeks to force through something, he does so for the sake of the kingdom of God. When he persecutes and crushes a fellowman, he does it thinking that the welfare of the church or of the Gospel or of Christianity demands it. The purely human desire for revenge and domination is thus represented under the guise of zeal for morality and the kingdom of God, for what is good and true. This is satanic. This is hypocrisy. However, the hypocrite will never be conscious of it so long as he remains in his unregenerate state.

The
Fundamental
Antithesis

Conversion — The New Birth

It would thus appear as if all the antitheses between Pharisaism and primitive Christian ethics rest upon one single fundamental antithesis, namely, that the Pharisaic manner of thinking is that man, by virtue of the endowment he has received from God, is capable of doing what is right, or, what is tantamount to it, that which is God's will. The primitive Christian view is that man must first experience an inner transformation, a recreation, receive a new life. The primitive Christion view, then, is epitomized in statements such as the following: "A good tree cannot bring forth evil fruit, neither can a corrupt tree bring forth good fruit" (Matt. 7:18); "Except a man be born again, he cannot see the kingdom of God" (John 3:3); "If any man be in Christ, he is a new creature; old things are passed away; behold, all things are become new." (2 Cor. 5:17)

It is easy, however, to reinterpret these New Testament utterances in a Pharisaic direction. This is also done to a great extent. Thus regeneration and the new birth are interpreted as if these were only figurative expressions for a transformation within the framework of the old life. When one already moves within a Pharisaic manner of thinking — and this is a common occurrence — these experiences have no reasonable meaning in their literal sense. One simply cannot conceive of a new birth, a new creation, a new life as anything but figurative expressions for a transformation. Characteristic is the expression "Begin a new life." By beginning a new life one by no means usually means that the person in question finds a new life in the New Testament sense, but does so by changing the manner in which he lives the same life that he has had since his birth. When one says "a new life," one really means nothing more than "a new manner of life," and one actually lacks the ability to recognize what a new life in the true sense of the word should be. *However, if one uses the expressions "new creation," "new birth," "a new life" in the sense of a transformed way of life, one moves entirely within the Pharisaic manner of thinking.* For Pharisaism "conversion," whereby man turns around from the direction leading away from God to the direction leading to God, is precisely to begin a new way of life by one's own ability, to change oneself, so that while one formerly acted in one manner, he now acts in another by his own strength.

An Analogy

This new way of life, however, is not the same as a new life in the New Testament sense. In order,

if possible, to demonstrate the great difference between these two concepts, let us use an analogy.
Of course, as in the case of all analogies, what is
compared does not correspond to every detail in
the analogy. One should be able to compare changing one's manner of life with an animal which is
trained so that, instead of acting according to its
"nature" or "instinct," it is induced to act and be-
have as a human being. A new life would, then,
be that a creature which formerly was an animal
actually receives human reason, human spirit, becomes a human being. The difference between the
old man and the new man in the New Testament
sense is at least as great as that between an animal
and a human being. The old man, according to the
primitive Christian interpretation, lacks something
fully as essential as what an animal lacks in comparison with a human being.

From the primitive Christian point of view, then,
the ethic which proceeds from man's determination
to become good, to do the will of God, and so forth,
and which imagines that everything is thereby in
good order, may be compared with the view which
declared that an animal trained to go dressed like
a human being and to go through human gestures
and actions thereby had become a human being.
Thus, from the point of view of primitive Christianity, the "righteous" individual is nothing but
a trained being who is not a whit nearer the true
righteousness, the true moral conduct of life, than

he who is a sinner, who has not been trained. It might also be questioned which of the two — the natural sinner and the one who has trained himself to act as a good man, that is, the "righteous" man — is the more valuable. This may be about as simple or as difficult to answer as the question as to which is the more impressive, a wild tiger at large or a trained tiger in a menagerie, a naked ape in the jungle or a dressed-up ape in a home. At this point the analogy falls short, since it is plain, according to the interpretation of primitive Christianity, that it is necessary that the one who is trained must abandon everything that he has gained through training in order to attain to the higher life; the "righteous" must be stripped of all "righteousness" in order to be saved.

On the other hand, this analogy might serve to illustrate why all who speak out of experience — who, in other words, have a past experience which they designate with such expressions as "new creation," "new birth," "illumination," or the like — always say that it is impossible to give an intelligible answer to the one who out of the old life asks, "What must I do to receive the new life?" One cannot give instruction as to any mode of procedure, as to anything that he should do within his own way of thinking; for every undertaking, every action, which takes place without this new creation having taken place is merely a change within the framework of the old and cannot, of course, bring forth the new. However, he is helped just as little by the answer that "he need do nothing," for an animal is not and does not become a human being by refraining from being trained anymore than by being trained. But inasmuch as a human being is able to understand that an animal lacks something essential which man possesses — if he is a man — so through this analogy one can, if not understand, nevertheless surmise, what separates the new from the old. The new man sees something, perceives something, possesses something the old man does not have. For the Christian this is something he has received through Christ, by having received Him in faith. Even this groping expression conveys no meaning to one who has not experienced it. But he who really desires to be extricated from the old life, to find the new life, to find the divine spark within him, appears to have found the answer to his question in the words "Seek, and ye shall find."

From this it follows that when one removes from Christianity the doctrine of Christ and the Spirit of Christ, making Him only an exalted teacher, then one has also abandoned the primitive Christian view and thereby holds the very opposite view: the Pharisaic.

This analogy can also demonstrate why the Christian ethic for him who has been born again, who has received the new vision, the new life, can abandon rules for life and conduct which often look exactly like the rules which are regarded as binding by the old man, who wishes to be righteous, but which he, on the other hand, never succeeds in following in the way of producing good results (good "fruits"). For the rules which Pharisaism regards as binding, and which it seeks to follow, are rules which do not flow out of the old life and are not ferreted out by the old man. These are, on the contrary, the expression of the divine life and its conditions.

The analogy referred to may possibly also illustrate why the new life on the whole has ethical principles and moral precepts. It is quite commonly said that since no one can become righteous or a good man by doing according to the Law, by observing the injunctions of the Moral Law, there can be no moral rules. They are then meaningless. Such reasoning is now applied to this analogy, as much as to say: Because a trained animal — an animal which acts like a human being, according to human rules — cannot become a human being by observing rules that apply to human beings, therefore neither can these rules have any significance for man himself. In other words, because the animal cannot become a human being, therefore neither can man fulfill his destiny and be a man!

From this it may be possible to gain a clearer understanding of the words of the Sermon on the Mount to which frequent reference has been made: "Every good tree bringeth forth good fruit; but a corrupt tree bringeth forth evil fruit. A good tree cannot bring forth evil fruit, neither can a corrupt tree bring forth good fruit. Every tree that bringeth not forth good fruit is hewn down and cast into the fire. Wherefore by their fruits ye shall know them" (Matt. 7:17-20). This Scripture passage belongs in the category of passages frequently interpreted and applied in such a manner as to lead to a meaning which is the very opposite of what the words actually say. It is said that these words of Jesus declare that one may see from a person's deeds whether he is a good man. For one can see whether he actually conducts himself and acts as he himself teaches, and whether in his external conduct he actually displays the manner of life that his code of morals, his religion, his Christianity prescribe. This interpretation, however, is the very opposite of what the above utterance from the Sermon on the Mount would say. For what these words actually declare is that one will not know a person by the deeds which he is seen to perform, but by the result, the "fruits," which his life produces. And then it often becomes evident that precisely he who, according to all appearances, consistently and constantly acts according to the precepts of the Law or religion by no means produces shining and beneficent deeds, but that everywhere, as a result of his activity, one can only see, besides his own success and the wielding of his power, corrupt fruits, nothing in which one can rejoice or which is a blessing to others. Thus, by considering the "fruits" of a "righteous" man's deeds one can see the proof of the correctness of the words, "a corrupt tree cannot bring forth good fruit." The fruits which are perceptible in man himself — in other words, not only in his works among others — are designated by Paul as "the fruits of the Spirit," that is, the fruits of the new life: "The fruits of the Spirit are love, joy, peace, long-suffering, gentleness, faith, meekness, temperance; against such there is no Law." (Gal. 5:22, 23)

The view of primitive Christianity is that the Law is holy, pure, and good. "Wherefore the Law is holy, and the commandments are holy and just and good," says Paul (Rom. 7:12). The Law has its origin in God. Pharisaism, however, according to the primitive Christian view, consists in wanting to attain the divine by means which are apart from God, in wanting to do God's will without inquiring about God. "We know that the Law is spiritual, but I am carnal, sold under sin" (Rom 7:14). Thus, it also becomes evident, according to the Gospel of John, that the "righteous," who with all their striving imagine that they are doing God's will, are powerless to do it; for when the voice of God speaks to them, they do not hear it; when God's messenger comes to them, they do not comprehend that he is from God. By very reason of their righteousness they reject the more bitterly that which is from God. The more divine it is, the more bitter is their opposition. This, according to the primitive Christian view, is the tragedy of the Pharisaic principle.

The Christian ethic, however, may be summed up in what St. Paul expresses thus: "I live; yet not I, but Christ liveth in me." (Gal. 2:20)